Hobby Farms® Presents · Volume 14K · 2015

Senior Associate Editor
Annika Geiger

Editor in Chief
Amy K. Hooper

Associate Art Director
Kari Keegan

Cover Design
Veronique Bos

Production Coordinator
Leah Rosalez

Contributing Photographers
Kevin Fogle, Fiona Green, Amy Grisak, Judith Hausman, Daniel Johnson, Kyra Kirkwood, Patricia Lehnhardt, Shannon O'Neill Creighton, Jen Nathan Orris, Alexander Small, Bonnie Sue, Terry Wild

Editorial, Production and Corporate Office
3 Burroughs
Irvine, CA 92618-2804
949-855-8822
fax: 949-855-3045

Sales Offices
500 N. Brand Blvd., Ste. 600
Glendale, CA 91203
213-385-2222
fax: 213-385-0335

477 Butterfield, Ste. 200
Lombard, IL 60148
630-515-9493
fax: 630-515-9784

COOKING WITH EGGS is published by I-5 Publishing, 3 Burroughs, Irvine, CA 92618-2804. Corporate headquarters is located at 3 Burroughs, Irvine, CA 92618-2804.

Imagination • Innovation
Insight • Inspiration • Integrity

MARK HARRIS, Chief Executive Officer; NICOLE FABIAN, Chief Financial Officer; KIM HUEY-STEINER, Chief Sales Officer; JUNE KIKUCHI, Chief Content Officer; BETH FREEMAN REYNOLDS, Vice President, Consumer Marketing; JENNIFER BLACK, General Manager and Vice President, Digital; MELISSA KAUFFMAN, Senior Editorial Director; LISA MACDONALD, Marketing Director; LAURIE PANAGGIO, Multimedia Production Director; CHRISTOPHER REGGIO, Book Division General Manager; CRAIG WISDA, Controller; CHARLES LEE, IT Director; CHERRI BUCHANAN, Human Resources Director

Reasonable care in handling photographs and written submissions will be taken, but COOKING WITH EGGS assumes no responsibility for lost or damaged material. © 2015 by I-5 Publishing LLC. All Rights Reserved. Reproduction of any material from this title in whole or in part is strictly prohibited.

Registration No.: R126851765
Part of the Hobby Farms® Presents Series
Printed in the USA

editor's

MW00636146

A Good EGG

BY ANNIKA GEIGER

"The way you make an omelet reveals your character." — Anthony Bourdain, American chef, author and television star

I don't know what Bourdain considers the "perfect" omelet. It seems every chef has a distinct opinion about how to cook eggs, however. Gordon Ramsay, another famous chef, is known for his scrambled eggs, to which he adds crème fraîche. To make hard-boiled eggs, Martha Stewart recommends letting the eggs sit in boiled water for exactly 12 minutes before draining. And celebrity chef Paula Deen — known for her Southern cooking but not its healthfulness — includes cream cheese and mayonnaise in her recipe for deviled eggs.

Fortunately, you don't have to be a famous chef to master the art of cooking eggs. Throughout this magazine, you will find more than 50 delicious recipes made with eggs. We've included all of the breakfast basics — scrambled eggs, omelets, eggs Benedict and more — as well as lunch foods such as soups, salads (with and without mayonnaise) and sandwiches. You'll also find recipes for eggy breads, appetizers, vegetarian dishes, gastropub-inspired fare, and desserts. There's something for every egg lover. Let's get cracking!

ALEXANDER SMALL

Cooking WITH Eggs

66

16

COVER IMAGE BY
Anna Hoychuk/
Shutterstock

86

JIRI HERA/SHUTTERSTOCK

GET TO KNOW Your Eggs

If you struggle to distinguish the differences between grocery-store eggs, you are not alone!

BY KEVIN FOGLE

Picking up a dozen eggs on the way home from work used to be a simple task. Today, the egg cooler at the local grocery store can be a confusing place for consumers who might become overwhelmed with a wide array of different egg-carton labels. These various labels contain a mix of officially regulated terminology and ambiguous or misleading jargon with terms such as organic, grade AA, free-range, natural, vegetarian diet and hormone-free. This article will provide useful clues to help you decipher egg cartons and become a more informed consumer about the size, type and freshness of the eggs that you purchase.

Making the Egg Grade

Have you ever wondered exactly what the phrases "grade A" or "grade AA" on egg cartons mean? The United States Department of Agriculture maintains egg-grading standards that recognize three grades of eggs based on internal as well as external inspections.

External inspections look at the shape of the egg and the condition of the shell. Internal inspections are done with a candling light to inspect the condition of the egg white and yolk and to check for abnormalities, like blood spots, without cracking open the egg.

Grade AA is the highest possible grade for an inspected egg. These nearly perfect eggs have unblemished shells; ideal shape; a firm white; a high, rounded yolk; and a very small air cell, meaning the egg is extremely fresh.

The most common eggs sold to consumers are **grade A**. This grade features the same exterior conditions as grade AA, but it allows a slightly larger air cell with a white that is only moderately firm.

The lowest USDA grade is **grade B**. Eggs with this classification might have lightly stained shells, the largest allowable air cell, partially flattened yolks and a thin white that spreads easily. These eggs are rarely seen in grocery stores, as most grade B eggs are bound for bakeries or large food-production facilities.

Only egg producers that obtain USDA monitoring services for their packing facility can be said to meet the above standards. Eggs without the USDA-grade shield on the carton are often monitored by various state regulatory bodies. It is important not to conflate egg grades with egg safety. The grade refers only to the physical condition of the egg, meaning that all grades are perfectly edible and nutritious, according to "Guide to Egg Carton Labels," an online publication from the Egg Nutrition Center and reviewed by the USDA.

KEVIN FOGLE

The American Egg Board says the large-sized egg is usually used in recipes. If you use another kind of egg, take that into consideration.

'Cracking' the Code

On every store-bought carton of eggs, you will find a sell-by or best-by date. But how do you know when and where your eggs were initially packed? This information is found in a stamped code on the carton — usually above, below or next to the sell-by date.

The code will look something like this hypothetical example: P1000 104. P1000 is the plant code, indicating the specific facility where the eggs were packed. All plant codes start with a P and end with a unique four-digit identifier. The three-digit number, 104, is the packing date for April 14th. Pack-date codes roll from 001, which represents January 1, all the way to 356, which is December 31.

The packing date does not guarantee freshness. Only the egg grade determines how fresh an egg is, with AA eggs as the most recently laid, according to the USDA's "Egg-Grading Manual." The exact layout of the code on your carton may appear slightly different or contain additional manufacturing information, but the plant code and packing date elements are always found within. These codes are also used for USDA-issued egg recalls, which are typically based on certain packing plants for a specified date range.

From Jumbo to Peewee: Understanding Egg Weight Classes

Sure, a large egg is bigger than a medium egg —but how much larger? Egg sizes are broken down into six weight classes ranging from jumbo, the largest, to peewee, the smallest.

Weight class is determined by the average weight of a dozen eggs: **jumbo (30 oz.), extra-large (27 oz.), large (24 oz.), medium (21 oz.), small (18 oz.)** and **peewee (15 oz.)**. Because the eggs are weighed by the dozen, the eggs within a carton often display some size variability.

If the carton displays a USDA shield for egg grades, it also means that the eggs were certified to meet the above weight-class standards. Without the USDA seal, egg weights might be monitored by state agencies or voluntarily checked by packers and producers, writes the USDA in its online publication "Shedding Light on the Grademark."

KEVIN FOGLE

The codes on an egg carton indicate the contents' freshness and where the eggs were packed.

All Natural, Hormone and Antibiotic-free Eggs

The terms "hormone-free," "antibiotic-free" and "all natural" commonly appear on egg-carton labels. These three phrases are intentionally misleading and primarily placed on cartons as marketing and sales tools, writes the Egg Nutrition Center in "Guide to Egg Carton Labels."

Although true, the claim that a carton of eggs contains no hormones is misleading, because the United States Food and Drug Administration does not permit the use of hormones in egg-producing chickens. The same is true for antibiotics, which are occasionally used for sick chickens. However, according to FDA regulations, eggs are not to be collected for human consumption during treatment.

Finally, the term "all natural" is perhaps the most dubious wording commonly found on egg-carton labels. According to the USDA, all fresh chicken eggs qualify as natural as long as they have not been altered in any way after laying.

The Chicken and the Egg Color

Brown chickens lay brown eggs, but so do some white-feathered breeds. Eggshell color is determined by breed, not the color of a bird's feathers.

At the grocery store, you will find both white and brown eggs. Both colors of eggs are essentially identical except for the pigmentation of the shell, according to the Egg Nutrition Center's "Guide to Egg Carton Labels." One color isn't inherently healthier than the other. Brown eggs often cost more, because the breeds that produce them require more feed or produce fewer eggs per bird.

Farm-fresh eggs are a completely different experience, where you can find a rainbow of colors from pale blue and olive-green eggs to speckled chocolate eggs. (More information about farm-fresh eggs is on page 16.) From my experience, small egg producers tend to raise a greater range of chicken breeds compared to commercial operations, which means that consumers can often find some delicious and unusually colorful egg options at local farmers markets.

Chicken Egg Anatomy

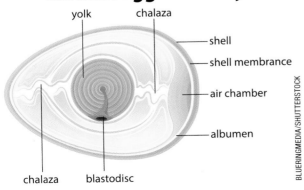

yolk — chalaza — shell — shell membrane — air chamber — albumen — chalaza — blastodisc

BLUERINGMEDIA/SHUTTERSTOCK

FIONA GREEN

There's More Than One Way to Cook an Egg

Scrambling: Because it requires so little skill, scrambling is many consumers' favorite way to serve eggs. Just heat a nonstick skillet with a little butter or fat, and add whisked eggs seasoned with salt, pepper and a dash of milk or cream. Using a spatula, keep the eggs moving until your desired doneness is reached.

Frying: To fry an egg, crack and gently place an egg in a sauté pan with preheated oil or fat. Cook over medium-low heat until the egg yolk is runny or well-set depending on your preference.

Basting: Basted eggs follow almost the same steps as fried eggs, except that when the egg is cooking in the pan, you must place a lid over the egg to catch the steam. The steam helps to quickly cook the egg yolk so the white does not overcook.

Hard-boiled: Perhaps the easiest method for preparing eggs, hard-boiling involves only a pan of water, while the entire egg stays in its shell. Bring a pan of water to a boil with the eggs in it. Remove from the heat, cover the pan, and let the eggs rest. After about 15 minutes (different cooks suggest different timeframes), transfer the eggs to an ice bath until cooled.

Poached: Fill a saucepan with water to within 1 inch from the lip. Add a pinch of salt and 1 Tbsp. vinegar, and warm over medium heat until the water is steaming. Crack an egg into a small ramekin or bowl, and stir the water, creating a slow, swirling current. Gently pour in the egg, and cook for approximately 3 minutes, or until the white is set but the yolk is still liquid. Carefully remove the egg with a slotted spoon. — K.F.

A Better Egg?

Vegetarian and omega-3 eggs refer to specialized eggs resulting from a targeted diet fed to laying hens. Vegetarian eggs are the product of chickens that consume a completely vegetarian diet, writes the Egg Nutrition Center in "Guide to Egg Carton Labels." These vegetarian eggs can be eaten by ovo-vegetarians (vegetarians who eat eggs) and people concerned with conventional commercial chicken feeds that can include objectionable proteins.

Omega-3 eggs have higher amounts of omega-3 fatty acids, which are emphasized in certain healthy diets. To increase the fatty acids in an egg, the hens enjoy an enhanced diet that typically includes flaxseed or sea-algae additives, which can double or triple the amount of omega-3s found in a regular egg, according to the Egg Nutrition Center in "Guide to Egg Carton Labels." As an added bonus, omega-3 eggs also tend to have higher levels of vitamin E, states the Flax Council of Canada.

The United States Department of Agriculture oversees the Egg Nutrition Center. Check out the ENC's **"Guide to Egg Carton Labels"** (www.eggnutritioncenter.org/wp-content/uploads/2012/04/ENC-Egg-Labeling-Guide-PDF-proof.pdf) for more information.

Eggs should be gathered within a few hours of when they were laid to stay fresh longer.

FIONA GREEN

According to the American Egg Board, the United States produces about 75 billion eggs per year in a wide variety of colors.

BONNIE SUE

An A-Peeling Process

The tedious task of peeling an egg deters some home cooks from making egg salad in large quantities. This is a task that takes either a lot of patience or a little creativity.

First, use older eggs; they are easier to peel. As eggs age, the moisture inside the shell evaporates. There is less egg volume, so there is more room between the egg and the shell. Clark suggests buying eggs at least a week before hard-boiling them.

Second, consider an egg's anatomy. There is an air cell in the roundest part of the egg (see page 7). Crack the egg here, and you'll have room to slide a spoon between the shell and the egg. Continue to slide the spoon along the surface of the egg toward the pointy end, and large pieces of the shell will crack off. You'll have some little pieces to deal with, too, but nothing like you do when you roll an egg on the countertop like you probably were taught to do when you were young. — Lisa Munniksma

The Two Frees: Free-range and Cage-free

"Free-range" and "cage-free" are two closely related terms that refer to the living conditions of laying hens. If an egg is cage-free, that means the production facility allows its hens to roam and roost freely in their poultry houses with regular access to food and water. Free-range production refers to cage-free hens that have some ability to get outside.

It is important to remember that cage-free and free-range labels on egg cartons are still only loosely regulated in the United States, writes Michael Ruhlman in "Egg: A Culinary Exploration of the World's Most Versatile Ingredient" (Little, Brown and Company), and living conditions for chickens vary significantly between different producers. For example, free-range chickens from a small, hobby egg producer might spend a significant amount of time outside in a large yard where they can roam and hunt insects, versus industrial production free-range hens that might be provided with limited access to small, paved outdoor porches, Ruhlman writes in his book.

AFRICA STUDIO/SHUTTERSTOCK

RA3RN/SHUTTERSTOCK

Large grocery stores can carry a dizzying array of eggs. Knowing the different types will make egg purchasing a lot easier.

It is important not to conflate egg grades with egg safety. The grade refers only to the physical condition of the egg, meaning that **all grades are perfectly edible and nutritious.**

Organic Eggs

When eggs are labeled "organic," it means that specific living conditions and dietary requirements have been met. Hens producing organic eggs must be free-range and cage-free. Their diet is the cornerstone of the organic claim; it means the chickens were fed a diet in which the grain and other individual ingredients were grown without the use of herbicides and pesticides, writes the Egg Nutrition Center in "Guide to Egg Carton Labels." You will often see bold claims about no hormones or antibiotics on these organic egg cartons — even though all eggs must meet this standard.

"Organic" is a term regulated by the USDA; as such, producers must display a USDA organic seal to indicate that their production facilities have been inspected and approved.

The wide variety of chicken eggs available in most grocery stores can make shopping for them a perplexing and bewildering experience. As a consumer, if you are truly concerned about the well-being, diet and living conditions of the hens producing your eggs, the best eggs you can purchase will likely be found at local farmers markets. Before purchasing, get to know the egg providers at the market, and ask them how their chickens are raised and which standards they follow. You can even take it one step further if you like by finding a farm-tour program in your area to get a first-hand perspective on local egg producers.

Kevin Fogle is freelance writer and photographer based in South Carolina.

A Veritable VARIETY

quail

chicken

So

you're planning on eating an egg for breakfast. Sound simple? Maybe not. Because we all love our chicken eggs, it's easy to forget that other types of domestic birds also produce tasty, nutritious eggs of various sizes and types.

The funny thing about eggs is that most people say they all taste about the same. If you prepare a dish using duck, quail or even emu eggs, guests will certainly notice subtle differences but usually will say something like, "It tastes like a chicken egg." This is actually a good thing, because it allows you to incorporate the more unusual types of eggs into recipes without worrying about drastic changes in flavor. You will, however, need to adjust the amounts!

Let's explore some of the accessible egg options.

Chicken
To help get our bearings, we'll examine the well-known chicken egg as a starting point. A standard 60-calorie chicken egg is about 2½ inches long,

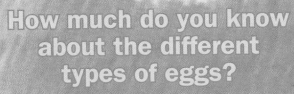

How much do you know about the different types of eggs?

BY DANIEL JOHNSON AND
SAMANTHA JOHNSON

weighs about 60 grams, and can be white or brown (or blue or green), depending on the breed of chicken. Sold by the dozen everywhere from convenience stores and farmers markets to grocery stores and Walmart, this is the egg that America loves most — and the only egg that many Americans have ever been exposed to. While chicken eggs have a lot going for them, they aren't the only egg out there, as we will soon see.

NUTRITION INFORMATION
Calories: 60 to 70
Protein: 6 grams
Cholesterol: 187 milligrams

Duck

A bit larger than chicken eggs, duck eggs tend to deliver a creamy, rich consistency. This creaminess is due to duck eggs' larger yolk-to-white ratio. It also means that they have a higher fat content than chicken eggs. Larger than chicken eggs, they naturally contain more calories per egg. Duck eggs feature a harder shell than chicken eggs and have a potentially longer refrigerated shelf life.

NUTRITION INFORMATION
Calories: 130
Protein: 9 grams
Cholesterol: 620 milligrams

PHOTOARTKATJA.COM/SHUTTERSTOCK

Pasture-raised chicken eggs often cost more than the kinds found at most grocery stores.

DANIELLE BALDERAS/SHUTTERSTOCK

JAMES CLARKE/SHUTTERSTOCK

Emu eggs can be found at some natural-foods stores for as much as $30 per egg!

Goose

Looking to take your egg size up a notch — without getting too large? Try goose eggs! Weighing in at about 5 ounces each, these eggs are equivalent to two or three large chicken eggs. Once you master the trick of cracking these giants (tapping them against a bowl won't cut it!), you'll find them a delight to eat.

Geese have a limited laying season of just a few months in the spring, and most birds lay only about 40 (give or take!) eggs per year.

NUTRITION INFORMATION
Calories: 265
Protein: 20 grams
Cholesterol: 1227 milligrams

Emu

With its delightful green coloring and whopping size, the hearty emu egg is both charming and delicious. Averaging about 5 to 6 inches long and weighing in at over 1 pound (!), the emu egg is the place to go when you're looking for fun and size.

But delivering such sizable goods takes time for a female emu to produce. She needs about three days to produce a single egg. On the other hand, an emu's egg makes up for the extra time needed by containing much more volume — about the equivalent of 10 chicken eggs! They also have a long refrigerated shelf life, thanks to their robust shells.

The egg-laying season for emus runs from about November to March (the summer months in their native Australia), which is another thing to keep in mind when purchasing eggs.

Have an artistic flair? Emu eggs are very popular with crafters due to their lovely color, size and durable shells.

Interestingly, according to the American Emu Association, emu eggs contain more "good" and fewer "bad" fats — 68% unsaturated and 31% saturated — than chicken eggs, which contain 63% unsaturated and 37% saturated fats.

NUTRITION INFORMATION
Calories: 60 to 75

Quail

But bigger isn't always better, is it? Maybe you don't want to go the super-size route of goose or emu eggs, but you'd still like to try something special. This diminutive, spotted egg is perfect if you'd like to experiment with a fun, unusual type of egg. At about 1 inch in length and 9 grams in weight, quail eggs are the smallest of the ones discussed here, but they are popular with chefs looking to make creative treats such as tiny, bite-sized deviled eggs.

NUTRITION INFORMATION
Calories: 14
Protein: 1.2 grams
Cholesterol: 76 milligrams

Where to Find Eggs

While chicken eggs can be found just about anywhere, it can be a challenge to locate some of the more unusual types. Perhaps you have friends or neighbors who keep unique birds and wouldn't mind having an outlet to sell excess eggs. Likewise, local farmers can be a great contact and — while it will depend on the individual situation and reputation — you can usually count on eggs from a local farmer to be fresh and flavorsome.

Quail eggs are featured in a variety of cuisines, including Japanese, Colombian and American.

OLYINA/SHUTTERSTOCK

Farmers' markets can be a **great source for eggs of all kinds,** although your success largely will depend on whether the egg you seek is currently in season.

CATLOOK/SHUTTERSTOCK

The Food and Agriculture Organization of the United States says China is the world's most prolific producer of chicken eggs.

Farmers markets can be another great source for eggs of all kinds, although your success often will depend on whether the egg you seek is currently in season.

If you can't find the variety you're looking for from these sources, you could try searching health-food or gourmet grocery stores, or hop online and look for sources (LocalHarvest.com is one option) for the eggs you're seeking. You can even purchase fresh quail eggs via Amazon.com and have them shipped right to your door.

If all else fails, you can look into the possibility of raising unique birds yourself — a potentially rewarding and fascinating experience! Raising ducks, geese — even emus! — can offer a ready source of fresh eggs that will provide endless quantities of delicious delight.

Daniel Johnson and Samantha Johnson are a brother-sister writing team and have collaborated on several books, including "The Beginner's Guide to Vegetable Gardening" (Voyageur Press).

Nest Box TO TABLE

Here's what you need to know about buying eggs directly from the farm, which differs from buying them at the grocery store.

BY LISA MUNNIKSMA

I know we just met, but let us rewind to four years ago when I disliked eggs very, very much. Something about them — taste, texture, smell — was just ... blegh. My appreciation for eggs hatched when I worked on a farm in Oregon that had a small flock of pasture-kept laying hens. I would see others on the farm eating some wonderful-looking egg-and-veggie scrambles for lunch, and I decided to try eggs again. The day I craved a fried-egg-and-tomato sandwich was a turning point in my life.

SUKHAREVSKYY DMYTRO (NEVODKA)/SHUTTERSTOCK

TFOXFOTO/SHUTTERSTOCK

Now I work on a farm that has a few hundred free-range laying hens. We sell the eggs at farmers markets and through a community-supported-agriculture program, and I still love eggs. You won't find me eating commercially produced eggs, though. There's something about the taste, texture and smell — plus the knowledge that I'm supporting a higher-animal-welfare product — of a farm-fresh egg that's better, in my nonscientific opinion.

If you're new to purchasing farm-fresh eggs, here's a primer for what to expect and how to find the best.

Egg Hunt

Farm-raised eggs are not often sold at the average supermarket. You'll likely have to go to a roadside farm stand, a farmers market, a natural-foods store or a neighbor who keeps chickens.

One purchasing option that's becoming more widely available is an egg CSA. Just like a vegetable CSA, you subscribe to the farm at the beginning of the season (usually during the spring), and each week, you receive a carton of fresh eggs. There's usually a small price break from retail, and you are guaranteed fresh eggs each week.

Pasture-raised chickens eat a variety of foods that often include what they've foraged.

FOTOKOSTIC/SHUTTERSTOCK

ALEXANDER SMALL

In rural communities, tasty eggs fresh from the farm are sometimes sold at roadside stands.

Eating Seasonally

It's easy to understand the concept of eating seasonally when it comes to vegetables; tomatoes grow in the summer, broccoli in the spring and fall, and so on. Similarly, most hens lay eggs year-round, but production is tied to daylight.

In industrial egg houses, hens don't experience daylight, only artificial light, so their laying cycles never change. On the other hand, you'll find a glut of farm-raised eggs that peaks in early summer and a scarcity by the time fall arrives. (This is when it's especially nice to be an egg CSA member, as mentioned on page 17.)

An Egg of a Different Color

In the grocery store, all of the eggs in the carton will be the same color: white or brown, depending on your preference. Purchasing eggs from a farm can result in a pastel rainbow of colors — white, brown, pink, blue, green — depending on the breeds of chickens that farm raises. The shell's contents are the same. (See page 7 for more information about eggshell colors.)

Financing the Farm Egg

Depending on where you live, a dozen eggs at the mega-grocery store might cost only $2.00. A dozen eggs from your local farmer might be $4.00; $6.00 if the chickens are pasture-raised; $8.00 if they're organic. The price difference between commercial eggs and local eggs lies in automation and economy of scale.

Pasture-raised eggs generally have a **bolder yolk color,** influenced by the range of foods that hens forage outdoors.

A Yolk's a Yolk

The egg yolk will look very different, as well. Pasture-raised eggs generally have a bolder yolk color that is influenced by the range of foods that hens forage outdoors.

You might find an egg with a double yolk, especially during the spring. You also might find a yolk with a blood spot. These are nothing to worry about; rather, they're just the way the egg was formed.

The difference goes beyond yolk appearance, though. A 2010 study by researchers at Pennsylvania State University found that eggs from pasture-raised hens have two times the amount of vitamin E, more than two times the omega-3 fatty acids, and a lower ratio of omega-6 to omega-3 fatty acids than conventionally produced eggs.

Sized Up

It's likely that you're buying unsized eggs from a farm source. In the grocery store, the cartons of jumbo, extra large, large and so on are determined by egg weight. Your small-scale egg farmer probably doesn't weigh each egg, so expect variations within a carton.

Egg's Rawest Form

Farm-raised eggs are, in almost all cases, not pasteurized. Pasteurization is the process of heating an egg to kill bacteria that might be inside. Recipes that call for raw or undercooked eggs should be prepared using pasteurized eggs or egg products — not farm-fresh eggs — according to the United States Department of Agriculture Food Safety and Inspection Service.

Feel Free to Ask

One nice aspect of buying eggs directly from the farmer is getting to know where your food comes from and how it's produced. Working at farmers markets, I have fielded a lot of questions about eggs. Here are a few to ask your egg farmer to ensure you've found a reputable source.

➤ HOW DO YOU RAISE YOUR CHICKENS?

Farm-raised eggs are not the same as pasture-raised eggs. A small-scale farmer can still use a confinement barn to keep his or her hens. You might ask if the chickens are:
- free-range or kept in cages
- pasture-raised or kept indoors
- organic according to the USDA's National Organic Program standards for producing eggs

If you prefer brown eggs, seek out farmers that own breeds like the Buff Orpington and the New Hampshire Red, both of which lay brown eggs.

TERRY WILD

Colorful eggs won't taste any different, but their beautiful hues bring a welcome change from brown and white.

LENA GABRILOVICH/SHUTTERSTOCK

without synthetic inputs. More information, including regulations, can be found at www.ams. usda.gov/AMSv1.0/nop

➤ WHAT DO THE HENS EAT?

Making eggs is an energy-intense process, so even pasture-raised hens require a grain ration to supplement the nutrition that they get from foraging. This is usually a mix of corn, soybean meal and minerals. These ingredients might be genetically modified or not. Premixed chicken feed might contain animal byproducts as a protein source. If any of these ingredients concern you, ask about them.

Pasture-based chickens are never truly "vegetarian-fed," as you see on the labels for some industrially produced eggs, because chickens are naturally omnivores. They are surprisingly good at catching — and eating — mice and snakes in the field.

➤ HOW OFTEN DO YOU COLLECT EGGS?

Daily — or more often — is the best answer, ensuring egg freshness and food safety. If a rooster is kept with the hens, daily egg collection will prevent a fertilized egg from developing.

➤ HOW OLD ARE THE EGGS YOU'RE SELLING TODAY?

According to the U.S. Food and Drug Administration, eggs remain fresh for four to five weeks, so judge the amount of time that it will take for you to use these eggs.

➤ HAVE THE EGGS BEEN WASHED?

Even if eggs appear clean, remember that they came from a farm environment. If your eggs have not been washed, do so at home before using them. The University of Nebraska-Lincoln has a home-egg-washing guide online at www. ianrpubs.unl.edu/sendIt/g1724.pdf

➤ ARE YOU INSPECTED BY THE EGG INSPECTOR?

Believe it or not, "egg inspector" is an actual state-government job. Laws governing the small-scale, direct-to-consumer sale of eggs vary by state. You can read the egg law from your state's Department of Food and Agriculture to learn more about what to expect from a farmer who is in line with the egg inspector, following the egg-sales and -safety rules.

Switching from grocery-store eggs to farm-fresh eggs takes some getting used to. Maybe it will change your egg-eating life, like it did mine, or you might want to go back to the ease and accessibility of the grocery-store variety. Now you're prepared for what to expect when you're ready to give farm eggs a try.

Freelance writer Lisa Munniksma has been working with pasture-raised laying hens since 2011. She blogs weekly about agricultural news and opinion at www.hobbyfarms. com/newshog and blogs occasionally about traveling and farming around the world at www.freelancefarmerchick.com

Experts in the United States recommend washing eggs before using them to prevent *Salmonella*.

BONNIE SUE

Pasture-based chickens are never truly "vegetarian-fed," as you see on the labels for some industrially produced eggs, because **chickens are naturally omnivores.**

EGGS ARE EXCELLENT

Recent research shows that eggs are healthier for you than previously thought.

BY LORI RICE

MORE THAN CAKE/SHUTTERSTOCK

Few foods have been involved in such health controversy as the humble egg. Due to the cholesterol contained in the yolk, the 2005 Dietary Guidelines for Americans stated that intake should be limited to four yolks per week. As a result, eggs became recognized for their negative qualities instead of the many beneficial nutrients they contain. Things are changing for eggs, though. Today they are gaining more attention for their role in a healthy diet.

The yolks contain many of the nutrients — such as vitamin D, calcium and iron — found in eggs.

BONCHAN/SHUTTERSTOCK

Healthy and Delicious

Eggs come loaded with valuable nutrients. The egg white contains the protein without the fat and cholesterol of the yolk, which is why many health-conscious people switched from using whole eggs to egg whites after the 2005 recommendations. The only problem: The yolk is where many of the vitamins and minerals are found.

Registered dietitian Rebecca Scritchfield, founder of Capitol Nutrition Group in Washington, D.C., sheds some light on the nutritional benefit of whole eggs. "One egg contains 6 grams of high-quality protein and all nine essential amino acids," she says. "Eggs are an excellent source of choline and selenium and a good source of high-quality protein, vitamin D, vitamin B_{12}, phosphorus and riboflavin. In addition, eggs are rich in the essential amino acid leucine, which plays a unique role in stimulating muscle protein synthesis." All of this nutrition comes with only about 70 calories for one large egg.

Another impressive trait: Eggs offer the highest biological value for protein, says Amber Pankonin, a Lincoln, Nebraska-based registered dietitian, adjunct professor and blogger at Stirlist.com. "The type of protein in eggs will be easily absorbed by the body. Protein is not only used to make new cells and help with cell recovery, but protein can help you to feel fuller longer," she says. "The choline in eggs plays a role in brain development and memory."

As research continues to evolve, these factors have returned eggs to the nutritional spotlight. They have ultimately led major health organizations and health professionals to change their recommendations for eating whole eggs.

As Scritchfield notes, "An egg a day is OK!" This is supported by the revised recommendations in the 2010 Dietary Guidelines for Americans, which state that healthy individuals can enjoy an egg daily and go so far as to suggest that one egg a day does not result in increased blood cholesterol levels.

"As new research on the benefits of protein becomes available," Scritchfield adds, "and the fact that dietary cholesterol is not viewed as negatively as in the past, eggs continue to shine as a nutrient-dense option in the diet."

> "The **choline** in eggs plays a role in brain development and memory."

As with all dietary recommendations, **turn to your doctor and a registered dietitian** for individual guidance.

While egg yolks carry many nutrients (page 24), egg whites contain protein and also form a healthy part of many individuals' diets.

ALEXANDRALAW1977/SHUTTERSTOCK

DANIEL JOHNSON

If the cholesterol still concerns you, take solace in the fact that the joint guidelines from the 2013 American College of Cardiology and American Heart Association do not recommend restricting dietary cholesterol. According to Scritchfield, this is consistent with many countries around the world that have removed daily cholesterol limits from their recommendations. Instead, they promote nutrient-dense foods, including eggs. As with all dietary recommendations, turn to your doctor and a registered dietitian for individual guidance. He or she can help you determine the right number of eggs, as well as the amount of dietary cholesterol, to eat based on your health status and current nutrition.

Incredibly Edible

Now that you can relax and enjoy your eggs, you might be wondering what the best way is to go about it. Both Scritchfield and Pankonin enjoy eggs and have plenty of suggestions for how to incorporate them.

"I usually eat eggs about two to three times per week," Pankonin says. "I enjoy them scrambled with a little bit of salt and pepper. I also enjoy making omelets loaded with lots of vegetables like spinach, tomatoes, onions and broccoli."

"You will always find a dozen or two of eggs in my fridge," Scritchfield says. "I will often fry up an egg and pair it with toast, avocado and hot sauce for a satisfying breakfast or lunch. I

Bacon makes a traditional — if not healthy — accompaniment to eggs.

Storing and Handling Eggs

According to Egg Safety Center, a consumer site provided by United Egg Producers, eggs should be refrigerated at a temperature of 45 degrees Fahrenheit or below in a carton in the coldest part of the refrigerator. Storing eggs in the door of your refrigerator can cause temperature fluctuations that promote the growth of bacteria. Eggs can be stored and used for three to five weeks after the day they are placed in the refrigerator, a timeframe supported by United States Department of Health and Human Services.

If you have traveled to Europe, you might have witnessed eggs stored at room temperature in the supermarkets. Varying storage practices around the world are directly related to differences in rules and regulations for the production and storage of eggs in each country. The major focus of all storage practices is controlling *Salmonella* contamination. Multiple organizations in the U.S., such as the United States Department of Agriculture and the Food and Drug Administration, collaborate to develop and enforce safety guidelines for egg production. The U.S. requires that eggs be washed, sanitized and refrigerated to reduce the risk of *Salmonella*. While some farmers choose to vaccinate hens for *Salmonella*, vaccinations are not mandated in the U.S.

European guidelines, such of those from the Food Safety Authority of Ireland, discourage egg washing because of evidence that this could spread *Salmonella*. Unlike in the U.S., vaccinating hens for *Salmonella* has been mandated for some time under regulating bodies, such as the British Egg Industry Council and its British Lion Quality Code of Practice.

All of these different regulations have led countries to produce and store eggs in ways that they feel are most effective to reduce *Salmonella* outbreaks. The safest practice is to follow the suggested guidelines for egg safety in the country where you buy your eggs. Always remember that once eggs are refrigerated, they must stay refrigerated regardless of their origin. The condensation that forms when a cold egg sits at room temperature can promote the spread of bacteria. — *L.R.*

also like to prep a large batch of egg salad at the beginning of the week to add to salads or make into sandwiches."

Now that you know not to believe all of those past myths surrounding this delicious, nutrient-packed food, take the lead of health experts, and appreciate eggs for all of their positive attributes. Eggs give a healthy boost to your breakfast, lunch or dinner.

Lori Rice is a freelance writer and nutritional scientist. She is the author of the health resource and cookbook "The Everything Guide to Food Remedies" (Adams Media). Lori shares her recipes, food photos and travel adventures on her blog, www. fakefoodfree.com

DAVID SALCEDO/SHUTTERSTOCK

The Egg-ceptional

EGG

Learn about alternative uses for this accessible item.

ARTICLE AND PHOTOS
BY FIONA GREEN

There

is no question about eggs' versatility. Nutritious and delicious, they can be used to create a variety of dishes that satisfy the whole family, and they are a key ingredient in many recipes ranging from appetizers and desserts to sauces and sides. Eggs also can be used to create a perfect glaze for pastries or edible paint for sugar cookies. While indispensable in the kitchen, the egg has many other uses in the home, which possibly makes it one of the most versatile food items in your kitchen.

Beauty Products

Eggs have been used in beauty treatments for hundreds of years, offering an inexpensive, natural alternative to pricey commercial products.

One of my personal favorites is the facial exfoliator. Mix together 1 egg yolk, ½ cup ground oats and 1 Tbsp. honey in a small bowl. Then apply liberally to your clean face, avoiding the mouth and eye areas. After 15 to 20 minutes, remove with a warm washcloth, pat dry, and apply your favorite moisturizer. Your skin will have a radiant glow and feel soft and healthy.

Egg whites might help reduce oily skin, tighten pores and control breakouts. Whisk 1 egg white until frothy, and then apply to your face. Leave on for 10 minutes, and rinse off with warm water.

Want to combat greasy hair? Apply a mixture of 1 egg white, 2 Tbsp. plain yogurt and 2 tsp. lemon juice to wet hair. Rinse off after 10 minutes, and shampoo and condition as usual.

Create your own conditioner by mixing 1 egg yolk with 1 Tbsp. coconut oil. Apply to your hair for 5 minutes; then rinse off, and wash hair as usual.

Cleaning Products

Don't throw out those eggshells! They can be recycled, too. If you are having trouble cleaning the insides of pots and pans, try using crushed eggshells to get the job done. Rub the shells into the stubborn burnt matter with a wet rag, and apply some elbow grease. Before long, your pots will regain their sparkle.

Gardening Aid

Eggshells can be used as miniature pots for starting seeds. Pierce a hole in the bottom of the half-shell for drainage, fill it with potting soil, and plant your seeds. When it is time to transplant, you can plant the shell in the garden.

Crushed eggshells add calcium to the soil and can help you grow prize-winning tomatoes and peppers! Place 1 Tbsp. crushed shells in the soil before planting to help prevent blossom-end rot (a disease that affects tomatoes, peppers and eggplant and causes the fruit to decay, beginning at the blossom end and spreading from there). Broken shells can be scattered around plants as a slug deterrent, too.

Keep broken eggshells in a jar filled with water, and use this nutrient-rich water for house plants. Alternatively, shells can be added to your compost pile along with other kitchen waste to contribute valuable nutrients and calcium to the soil. To avoid possible issues with bacteria, some experts recommend boiling the shells or baking them in the oven at 250 degrees Fahrenheit for at least 20 minutes. They should then be crushed to help decompose more quickly.

Hobbies and Art Projects

If you run out of paper glue for your art projects, try using egg whites as a temporary measure.

Save money by making customized paint with egg yolks and tempera pigment. Tempera paint is ideal for painting on inflexible surfaces like wood.

Did you know you can make your own sidewalk chalk using eggshells? Simply mix 2 tsp. flour with 2 tsp. hot water to form a thick paste. In a blender, crush 6 clean, dry shells to create a powder. Combine the powder with the flour mixture, and add a drop or two of food coloring if desired. Roll into a sausage shape, wrap in a paper towel, and leave to dry for a couple of days.

Eggshells also make excellent material for mosaic projects. Apply broken pieces to vases or jars to create beautiful, original works of art.

Children's Activities

Create a fun art project by hard-boiling eggs and inviting children to express themselves with colorful, crazy designs. Alternatively, you can organize an egg-on-a-spoon race, a juggling contest or a treasure hunt with numbered eggs hidden in the house or garden.

It's hard to believe that with just one box of eggs, you can make breakfast, glaze a pie, enjoy a facial, condition your hair, clean pots and pans, fertilize your vegetables, decorate a vase and keep your children busy. Now that's pretty egg-ceptional!

Fiona Green is a writer and photographer living in Keller, Texas. When she's not rescuing animals, running or creating chaos in the kitchen, she can usually be found working on some DIY project in her house or garden.

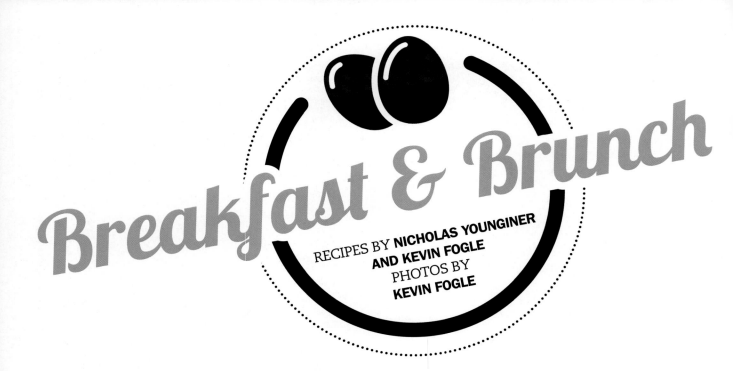

Breakfast & Brunch

RECIPES BY **NICHOLAS YOUNGINER AND KEVIN FOGLE**
PHOTOS BY **KEVIN FOGLE**

When you think about breakfast and brunch dishes, eggs are almost always a fundamental ingredient. The following six recipes are classic morning meals that highlight eggs in both traditional and unexpected ways from a perfect French tri-fold omelet to a savory Monte Cristo sandwich featuring herbed French toast. Each of these recipes will brighten your breakfast table with a burst of flavor.

Perfect Scrambled Eggs with Chives and Sage

When combined with the toast or side of your choice, scrambled eggs make a hearty, comforting breakfast.

Makes 4 servings

½ Tbsp. butter
4 whole sage leaves
8 eggs
5 Tbsp. whole milk or heavy cream
½ tsp. salt
¼ tsp. black pepper
2 Tbsp. chives, finely chopped

1 Heat a nonstick skillet over medium heat. Melt the butter in the pan, and add the sage leaves. Fry until the leaves are translucent and crisp. Leaving the butter in the pan, remove just the sage leaves, and set them aside. Reduce the heat to low.

2 In a large bowl, whisk the eggs until the whites and yolks are completely blended and the eggs have lightened in color to a pale yellow (about 1 minute). Stir in the milk or cream, salt, pepper and chives.

3 Pour the egg mixture into the heated pan. Continuously stir until the eggs are almost cooked, but there is still some liquid egg in the pan. Remove the pan from the heat, and continue to stir just until the eggs are cooked but not dry. Serve immediately garnished with the fried sage leaves.

Tri-fold Omelet with Sweet Ham and White Cheddar

American omelets are typically folded in half before serving. The three folds in this recipe make it French-inspired. Any method will do, however.

Makes 1 omelet

1 tsp. + 2 tsp. olive oil
3 eggs
2 Tbsp. whole milk or heavy cream
½ tsp. salt
½ tsp. ground black pepper
1 Tbsp. yellow onion, chopped into ⅛-inch dice
3 Tbsp. sweet ham, chopped into ¼-inch dice
4 Tbsp. white Cheddar, grated

1 Heat a nonstick pan over medium-low heat with 1 tsp. olive oil.

2 While the pan heats, beat the eggs in a bowl until the whites and yolks are completely blended, giving the eggs a pale yellow color. Stir in the milk or cream, salt and pepper, and set aside.

3 Into the pan, add the onion, and sauté until the pieces are slightly browned and translucent. Remove from the pan, and set aside.

4 Replace the pan over medium-low heat, and add the remaining olive oil. Heat the pan until the oil shimmers.

5 Once heated, pour the egg mixture into the pan, and let it sit for approximately 1 minute. As the bottom of the omelet cooks, lift and rotate the pan so the liquid egg on top flows around the edges of the pan and cooks. Lift the edge of the cooked egg to allow the remaining liquid egg to pool underneath. Repeat this process until there is no longer pooled liquid egg on top, but the egg is not completely dry. Have a serving plate ready.

6 Place the ham, cooked onion and cheese in a line across the egg within the top one-third of the cooked egg in the pan (the portion farthest away from you). Fold the far edge of the egg over the ingredients.

7 Lift the pan over the serving plate, and push the omelet out of the pan while simultaneously rolling it so it folds over on itself, with the seam facing downward on the plate. Serve the omelet immediately.

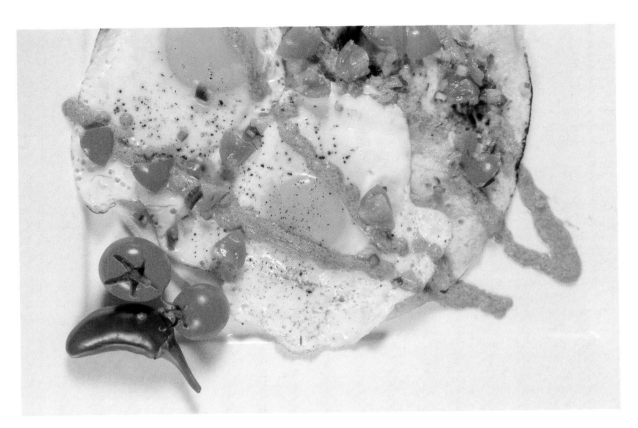

Huevos Rancheros with Spinach and Roasted Poblano Verde Sauce

This favorite Mexican dish is often seen on the menu at restaurants that specialize in breakfast foods.

Makes 4 servings

3 poblano peppers
1 cup chicken stock
1 tsp. cumin
2 cups raw spinach
1 Tbsp. garlic, minced
1 cup plain Greek yogurt
1 cup sour cream
1 Tbsp. olive oil
4 eggs
salt and pepper to taste
4 flour tortillas
1 large tomato, diced
¼ cup red onion, finely diced
4 sprigs cilantro, chopped

1 Using a pair of tongs, hold the poblano peppers over the open flame of the gas stove. Rotate every 2 minutes until the skins are blackened and charred.

2 Once charred, put the poblano peppers in a bowl, and cover with plastic wrap. Set aside for 10 minutes until cooled. Once cooled, rub off the charred skins, and remove the tops and seeds.

3 Place a medium-sized pot over medium heat, and add the chicken stock, cumin, spinach and garlic. Heat until beginning to steam slightly and the very edges of liquid bubble slightly.

4 In a blender, combine the heated contents of the pot, poblanos, yogurt and sour cream. Blend until smooth, and set aside the sauce. **Note:** Leave a small gap between the blender body and top so that some heat can escape while blending.

5 Bring a nonstick skillet to medium-low heat. Add the olive oil, and crack the eggs into the pan. Season with salt and pepper, and place a lid on the skillet. After the whites have set and the yolks are a deep yellow color and have a gel-like consistency (about 4 minutes), remove the eggs from the pan, and set aside.

6 Toast or warm the tortillas. Once crisp and browned, remove the tortillas, and assemble each dish with 1 tortilla topped with a cooked egg. Finish with the sauce, and garnish with tomato, red onion and cilantro.

Eggs Benedict with Herb-poached Eggs and Hollandaise Sauce

Eggs Benedict remains a popular, well-loved breakfast dish. Try a twist on the traditional recipe by adding fresh herbs to the poached eggs.

Makes 4 servings

pinch of salt
1 Tbsp. apple cider vinegar
2 sprigs thyme
1 sprig rosemary
2 bay leaves
8 eggs (4 whole and 4 to be separated)
1 Tbsp. lemon juice
1 Tbsp. water
1 stick butter (8 Tbsp.), melted
pinch of salt
2 English muffins, split in half
4 slices sweet ham

1 Into a medium-sized saucepan, pour water to within 1 inch from the lip of the pan. Place the pan over medium heat, and add the salt, vinegar, thyme, rosemary and bay leaves. Heat the water and infuse it with the herbs.

2 Crack 4 eggs into a small ramekin, and set aside.

Time-saving tip: Fry the eggs instead of poaching them.

3 Once steam begins to rise from the water, remove the herbs. Stir the water to create a slow, swirling current, and gently pour in the eggs, one at a time. Allow them to cook until the egg whites are set but the yolk is still liquid (approximately 3 minutes). Gently remove the eggs from the water with a slotted spoon, and set aside.

4 Separate the remaining 4 eggs, reserving all of the yolks and 2 whites.

5 Place a small saucepan half-filled with water over medium heat, and bring it to a simmer.

6 In a glass bowl that sits stably in the saucepan, add the egg yolks and lemon juice, and stir to combine. Place the bowl over the saucepan containing simmering water, making sure the water does not actually touch the glass bowl.

7 Whisk until the yolks turn a light yellow color and thicken slightly. Every 30 seconds, remove the bowl from the heat so the yolks don't overcook.

8 Once the yolks are pale yellow and thickened, remove the bowl from the heat, and slowly stream in the melted butter while continuously whisking to incorporate the butter. Season with salt to taste, and set aside.

9 In a blender, combine the egg yolks and lemon juice. Pulse for 15 seconds or until the yolks and lemon juice are thoroughly mixed and lightened in color.

10 Heat the water in the microwave for 1 minute. Turn on the blender containing the egg yolk and lemon-juice mixture, and stream in the hot butter. Then add the hot water. Add the salt, and pulse to combine. **Note:** The egg yolks will not be fully cooked; use pasteurized eggs if desired. (See page 19 for more information.)

11 Toast the English muffins. Meanwhile, heat the ham in a pan over medium heat until hot and slightly browned.

12 To serve, stack a slice of ham on half of an English muffin, and place the poached egg on the ham. Pour the Hollandaise sauce over the top of the stack. Serve immediately.

Thyme-infused Sourdough Monte Cristo Sandwich with Sweet Ham and Gruyère Cheese

The American version of the French croque monsieur, the Monte Cristo elevates the simple ham-and-cheese sandwich to a breakfast or brunch delicacy.

Makes 4 sandwiches

4 eggs
1 cup milk
4 sprigs lemon thyme leaves, roughly chopped (regular thyme can be used, too)
salt and pepper to taste
8 slices sourdough bread
½ Tbsp. butter
16 slices sweet ham
2 cups Gruyère cheese, shredded

1 Into a large bowl, crack the eggs, and whisk until blended. Pour in the milk, and add the thyme, salt and pepper. Whisk until thoroughly mixed.

2 Soak the slices of sourdough in the egg mixture, turning a few times until the bread is saturated.

3 Remove the bread from the mixture, and set aside. Meanwhile, bring a very large pan to medium heat.

4 Once the pan is heated, add the butter, let it melt entirely, and place the egg-soaked bread slices in the pan. Cook until the bread looks browned on both sides and cooked through in the middle (about 5 to 7 minutes total cooking time).

5 Meanwhile, turn on the oven's top broiler setting. Once the bread is cooked, remove the slices from the pan, and place 4 of them on a baking sheet. On these slices, place the ham (4 slices per sandwiches) and some grated cheese.

6 Melt the cheese under the broiler (about 2 to 3 minutes). Remove from the oven, and top the sandwiches with the remaining cooked sourdough slices. Serve hot.

Steak and Yorkshire Pudding with Sweet and Savory Cherry Compote

Steak and eggs (in this case, in the form of Yorkshire puddings) make the perfect filling breakfast.

Makes 4 servings

4 Tbsp. + 1 Tbsp. vegetable oil
3 eggs
¾ cup milk
¾ cup flour
½ tsp. salt
1 tsp. black pepper
½ cup grated Parmesan cheese
1 medium yellow onion, chopped into ⅛-inch dice
2 cups cherries, pitted and roughly chopped
1 sprig rosemary
1½ Tbsp. sherry vinegar
2 Tbsp. brown sugar

4 7- to 8-oz. hanger steaks (or any preferred cut)
salt and pepper to season
1 Tbsp. butter

1 Preheat the oven to 450 degrees Fahrenheit. Into 8 sections of a muffin tin, pour ½ Tbsp. of vegetable oil in each, and place in the oven for 6 to 7 minutes until the oil is hot.

2 In a mixing bowl, whisk the eggs and milk until blended and slightly foamy. Stir in the flour, salt, pepper and Parmesan.

3 Remove the tin from the oven, and pour batter into each muffin section until halfway filled. The batter should bubble and begin to fry immediately once added.

4 Place the muffin tin in the oven for 15 to 20 minutes, or until all of the puddings puff and look browned. Remove from the oven, and let cool.

Time-saving tip: Buy frozen Yorkshire puddings in British specialty stores, or substitute with frozen popovers.

5 Place a saucepan over medium heat. When the pan is hot, add 1 Tbsp. oil and the onion. Sauté until browned and translucent.

6 Add the cherries and rosemary, and cook for 4 minutes or until some of the liquid from the cherries cooks off and the fruit softens. Remove the rosemary sprig.

7 Pour in the sherry vinegar, and stir to loosen any bits that have cooked to the bottom of the pan. Add the brown sugar, and stir. Cook for about 3 minutes or until the sugar has dissolved and the compote thickens slightly. Set aside.

8 Remove the steaks from the refrigerator about 30 minutes before cooking to allow them to warm slightly. Season liberally with salt and ground black pepper.

9 Place a pan over high heat. Add the butter. Once the butter is melted, place the steaks in the pan, and cook for 3 to 4 minutes on each side for medium rare.

10 Remove the steaks from the pan, and let them rest for 5 to 10 minutes before serving. Plate each steak with a Yorkshire pudding and a serving of cherry compote.

Nicholas Younginer is a trained chef and nutritional anthropologist based in South Carolina. Kevin Fogle is a freelance writer and photographer also located in South Carolina.

Omelets

RECIPES AND PHOTOS BY
FIONA GREEN

An omelet is an easy, delicious meal to throw together. Whether you fry or bake it in the oven, the preparation is quick, and the sky's the limit when it comes to fillings.

When stove-top cooking an omelet, use a nonstick pan and clarified butter or ghee to grease the pan. That produces a tastier, less oily omelet. Prepare the filling ingredients in advance so they are ready to be added when the eggs are cooked. Your eggs will cook more evenly if you bring them to room temperature first. Place them in a bowl of warm water for 5 minutes prior to use.

Omelet with Smoked Salmon and Cream Cheese

There is something very decadent about eating smoked salmon and cream cheese for breakfast, and the combination begs to be savored. For aesthetics, the omelet in this recipe is rolled or tri-folded like a French omelette as opposed to the traditional American omelet, which is filled and then folded in half.

Serves 1

Honey Mustard Dressing (makes several servings)
3 Tbsp. honey
2 Tbsp. mustard
4 Tbsp. olive oil
3 Tbsp. red wine vinegar
pinch of salt
pinch of pepper

1½ oz. smoked salmon, cut into small pieces
2 Tbsp. cream cheese
3 green onions, finely chopped
2 tsp. fresh dill, finely chopped
1 tsp. clarified butter
2 eggs
1 egg white
1 Tbsp. water
salt and pepper to taste

1 Prepare the dressing: Place all of the ingredients in a small jar, and shake until combined. Refrigerate until ready to use.

2 Place the salmon, cream cheese, green onions and dill on a plate, and set aside.

3 Add the clarified butter to an 8-inch frying pan and heat, moving the pan to coat its base.

4 In a small bowl, whisk the eggs, egg white, water, salt and pepper.

5 Once the butter becomes hot, pour in the eggs. Cook over medium heat, moving the eggs around the pan with a rubber spatula for about 1 minute to distribute evenly and allow the uncooked egg to pass underneath. Cook for 2 to 3 minutes until the omelet is done, taking care not to overcook.

6 Spoon the filling into the middle. Lift 1 side of the omelet toward the center to cover the ingredients, followed by the other side. Carefully transfer to a serving plate, and garnish with dill. Serve with the honey mustard dressing.

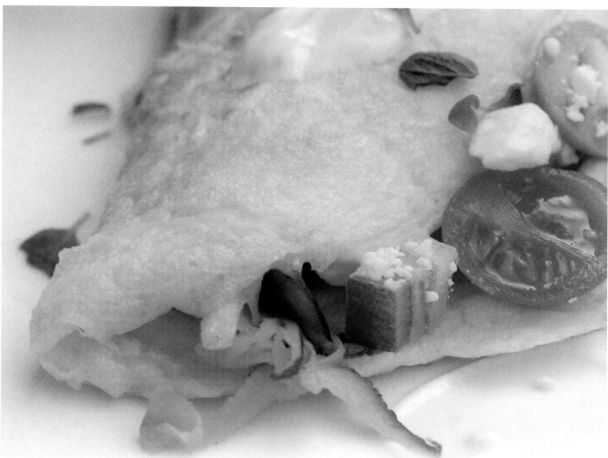

Mediterranean Omelet

The inspiration for this omelet came from trips to Greece, where the vegetables always tasted like they had just been picked. This recipe uses fresh oregano, but feel free to experiment with other herb(s). For a satisfying meal, add the dressing and a baguette.

Serves 2

Cucumber Yogurt Dressing
1 cup thick Greek yogurt
¼ cup grated cucumber
2 tsp. fresh dill, chopped
½ tsp. minced garlic
1 Tbsp. lemon juice
1 Tbsp. olive oil
pinch of salt
pinch of pepper

¼ cup crumbled feta cheese
10 cherry tomatoes, halved
10 olives, sliced
1 Tbsp. red onion, finely chopped
½ small zucchini, thinly sliced
1 tsp. fresh oregano
4 eggs

2 egg whites
2 Tbsp. water
2 tsp. clarified butter

1 Prepare the dressing: In a bowl, mix the yogurt, cucumber, dill, garlic, lemon juice, olive oil, salt and pepper. Adjust the amount of dill to taste. Refrigerate until ready to use.

2 Next, prepare your filling. In a bowl, mix the feta, tomatoes, olives, red onion, zucchini and oregano, and set aside.

3 Whisk the eggs and egg whites with the water in a small bowl until light and fluffy.

4 Heat the clarified butter in a 12-inch frying pan over medium heat. When the butter is hot, pour the eggs into the pan. Using a rubber spatula, stir gently for 1 minute to allow the uncooked egg to pass underneath. Then cook for 2 more minutes.

5 Arrange the fillings on 1 side of the omelet; then fold over the top to form a half-moon shape, and cook for 30 seconds. Remove from the heat, cut in half, and serve immediately.

Baked Veggie and Goat Cheese Omelet

When you are preparing breakfast for a group, consider making a baked omelet. The preparation is easy, leaving more time to socialize with your guests.

Serves 4

½ cup (about 10) grape or cherry tomatoes, halved
⅓ cup shelled edamame
¾ cup crumbled goat cheese
⅓ cup sundried tomatoes
½ red pepper, chopped
1 shallot, chopped
¼ cup parsley, chopped
8 eggs
4 Tbsp. water
4 Tbsp. whipping cream
pinch of salt
pinch of pepper
pinch of paprika
¼ cup grated Gruyère cheese or another strong
  cheese

1 Preheat the oven to 375 degrees Fahrenheit.

2 Begin by preparing the filling. In a bowl, mix the tomatoes, edamame, goat cheese, sundried tomatoes, red pepper, shallot and parsley. Set aside.

3 In a separate bowl, whisk the eggs with the water, cream, salt, pepper and paprika.

4 Fold the vegetable filling into the egg mixture.

5 Pour the mixture into a greased 8-inch square casserole dish or a 9½-inch pie pan. Cook for 20 to 25 minutes or until a toothpick inserted into the omelet comes out clean.

6 Remove from the oven, and serve with a sprinkling of cheese and hot sauce.

Meat Lover's Omelet

In this recipe, an omelet with sausage, bacon and potatoes is oven-baked to provide a satisfying breakfast. Make the dish your own by experimenting with different sausages and cheeses.

Serves 4

8 small red potatoes, unpeeled
2 slices bacon
¼ small onion, sliced
6 oz. smoked sausage, sliced
1 tsp. minced garlic
1 tsp. butter
8 eggs
4 Tbsp. water
½ tsp. chipotle pepper flakes
1 cup manchego cheese, grated
salt and pepper to taste

1 Boil the potatoes for about 15 minutes or until soft but not mushy.

2 Meanwhile, cook the bacon until slightly crispy. Cut into small pieces, and set aside in a bowl. Add the onion and sausage.

3 When the potatoes are ready, remove them from the pot, and mash with a fork. Add the garlic and butter.

4 Evenly spread the potatoes over the bottom of an 8-inch square casserole dish or a 9 ½-inch pie pan. Cover the potatoes with a layer of the sausage, onion and bacon mixture. Top with half of the grated cheese. Preheat the oven to 375 degrees Fahrenheit.

5 Whisk the eggs with water in a bowl until light and fluffy. Pour the eggs over the sausage mixture, and bake for 25 minutes. Remove from oven, cover with remaining cheese, and return to oven for 5 minutes. Serve with salsa.

Fiona Green is a photographer and writer living in Keller, Texas, who balances her love of creating and eating delicious food with competitive running.

RECIPES AND PHOTOS BY **AMY GRISAK**

Eggs are exceptional when it comes to one-pan meals that are hearty and easy to create for a weekend brunch or midweek meal. Whether baking or cooking them on the stove, egg skillet dishes bring together everything you need for a balanced meal, including plenty of vegetables. The best thing about these dishes is their versatility. They are perfect for seasonal menus, allowing you to use what is freshest and tastiest at any time of the year. You can experiment with adding various meats and cheeses. Every meal will be different yet enormously satisfying.

Spring Baked Eggs

There's nothing like fresh, early vegetables and eggs to celebrate spring. When you would rather enjoy the warming days instead of spending time in the kitchen, take advantage of the freshest vegetables to create this filling and delicious single-skillet meal.

Serves 2 to 4

1 Tbsp. olive oil
1 Tbsp. butter
8 to 10 red new potatoes, scrubbed and sliced ⅛-inch thick
4 green onions, washed and finely chopped
1 handful asparagus, washed and chopped into ½-inch
    pieces (1 heaping cup)
1 cup chopped spinach, washed and patted dry
¼ cup chopped Italian parsley
6 oz. precooked ham, cut into ½-inch cubes
salt and pepper to taste
4 eggs

1 Preheat the oven to 400 degrees Fahrenheit.

2 To an ovenproof, 8-inch skillet, add the olive oil, butter and potatoes. Coat the potatoes with the oil.

3 Place the pan in the oven, and bake for 25 minutes, occasionally turning the potatoes so they cook evenly.

4 Add the green onions, asparagus, spinach, parsley and ham. Bake for about 10 minutes, stirring halfway through. Add salt and pepper to taste.

5 Once the potatoes and vegetables are cooked and the ham is heated through, make 4 slight indentations in the potatoes and vegetables. Crack an egg into each indentation.

6 Bake for 10 minutes or until the eggs are done to your preference.

Harvest-time Egg Skillet

The end-of-the-summer bounty provides an incredible array of vegetables. This combination of seasonal flavors with eggs is the perfect way to make a hearty breakfast, or truly any meal of the day, in less than 45 minutes.

Serves 4

2 Tbsp. butter
1 Tbsp. olive oil
3 to 4 Yukon Gold potatoes, washed, peeled and chopped into ¼- to ½-inch pieces
¾ sweet pepper, cut into ½-inch pieces
1 leek, washed and sliced
1 cup chopped zucchini (or any other summer squash)
½ cup sun-dried tomatoes, soaked and sliced
1 cup kale, washed and finely chopped
½ tsp. dried thyme or 1 tsp. fresh
salt and pepper to taste
6 eggs
1½ cups shredded Cheddar cheese

1 To a 12-inch skillet, add the butter and oil, followed by the potatoes. Cook the potatoes over the medium-heat stove for about 10 minutes.

2 Add the pepper, leek, zucchini, tomatoes and kale. Then add the thyme, salt and pepper. Continue to cook until the potatoes and vegetables are cooked — roughly 15 more minutes.

3 In a bowl, scramble the eggs. Pour over the top of the potato and vegetable mixture. Stir until cooked through.

4 Top with shredded Cheddar cheese. Let the cheese melt before serving.

Freelance writer Amy Grisak relies on her family's half-dozen hens to supply the eggs she needs for quick meals throughout the year. Follow her gardening, cooking and hiking adventures at thebackyardbounty.com

Breads

RECIPES AND PHOTOS BY
PATRICIA LEHNHARDT

When included in bread dough, eggs add richness, act as a leavening agent to help the bread rise, and contribute lecithin for a good crumb consistency. Now, bread added to eggs is another story. It tastes like pure bliss in the form of decadent French toast or soft dinner rolls repurposed with quiche filling. Leftover bread never had it so good when matched up with eggs.

French Toast

This favorite breakfast is dressed up with a coating of breadcrumbs and almonds to add a crunchy note to its custardy center. Fresh berries complete the plate for this indulgence.

Serves 4

4 eggs
1 cup half-and-half
½ tsp. almond extract
¼ tsp. freshly grated nutmeg
pinch of salt
4 slices egg bread, sliced 1 inch thick
2 cups fresh, coarse breadcrumbs
   (instructions appear to the right)
¼ cup sliced almonds
¼ cup butter

1 In a 9-by-13-inch baking dish, whisk the eggs, half-and-half, almond extract, nutmeg and salt. Soak the bread slices in it for 5 minutes on each side.

2 In a wide dish, combine the breadcrumbs and almonds. Press the crumb mixture onto the soaked bread so it adheres to both sides.

3 Melt the butter in a large skillet, and fry the bread over medium-low heat until golden-brown on both sides and set in the middle. Serve with maple syrup.

To make the breadcrumbs: Cut the ends from the loaf of egg bread, and tear into large pieces. Place in a food processor, and pulse until you have coarse crumbs. You will need 2 cups here.

Old-fashioned Dinner Rolls

The dinner table seems incomplete without these egg-rich soft rolls. For equally great sandwich buns, divide the dough into 8 portions, and place them 2 inches apart on the baking sheet. Brush with an egg-wash, and sprinkle with sesame seeds.

Makes 16

1 large (8 oz.) russet potato
1 cup water
2 eggs
¼ cup sugar
1½ tsp. salt
6 Tbsp. melted butter
1 Tbsp. active-dry yeast
4½ cups all-purpose flour, divided

1 Peel the potato, and cut it into 1-inch pieces. Place the pieces in a saucepan, and add the water. Bring to a boil, lower the heat, and simmer until the pieces are tender — about 15 minutes. Drain the water into a measuring cup; you will need ¾ cup. (Add more water if necessary.) Mash the potato, and measure out 1 cup. Cool to room temperature.

2 In a large mixing bowl, combine the potato, ¾ cup potato cooking water, eggs, sugar, salt, butter, yeast and 2 cups flour. Beat until smooth. Slowly add the remaining flour to create a soft, sticky dough. Cover with a cloth. Let rise until double in size — about 1 ½ hours.

3 Grease 2 9-inch pie pans. Dump the dough onto a floured surface, and divide into 16 portions. Roll each piece into a ball, pulling the edges under and creating a surface tension that will keep the roll smooth. Pinch together the dough on the bottom as you work.

4 Place 8 rolls in each pie pan. Cover with a towel, and let rise until puffed — about 1 hour. Preheat the oven to 375 degrees Fahrenheit.

5 Bake for 25 minutes or until golden.

Challah

Challah is a rich, eggy bread with distinctive flavor that is enhanced by multiple risings. Traditionally braided, the loaf looks beautiful with a crisp, shiny crust and poppy seeds scattered on top.

Makes 1 loaf

2 tsp. active-dry yeast
2 tsp. sugar
¾ cup warm water (110 degrees Fahrenheit)
¼ cup canola oil
3 large eggs, lightly beaten
¼ cup sugar
1½ tsp. fine sea salt
4 cups all-purpose flour, divided, plus up to ¼ cup

Egg wash
1 large egg
1 Tbsp. poppy seeds

1 In a large bowl, stir together the yeast, sugar and water. Set aside for 5 minutes or until foamy.

2 Stir oil, eggs, sugar, salt and 3 cups flour into the yeast mixture to form a soft, sticky dough. Work in the remaining 1 cup of flour with your hands.

3 Dust the work surface with 1 or 2 tablespoons additional flour. Knead until smooth, about 5 to 6 minutes, adding only as much flour as needed to prevent it from sticking to the surface.

4 Clean and oil the bowl. Place the dough in the bowl, turn to coat, cover with a towel, and let rise until double in size — about 1½ hours.

5 Punch down, and let rise again for 1½ hours. Alternatively, you can refrigerate the dough for a long, cold overnight rise, which makes managing the timing easier and adds flavor.

6 If you refrigerated the dough, remove it from the refrigerator for 1 hour before using. Divide into 3 portions, and roll each into a rope of 1 inch wide and 18 to 20 inches long. Braid the 3 ropes together, pinching the ends and tucking them under.

7 Place on a parchment-lined baking sheet. Cover with a towel, and let the dough rise for 1½ hours.

8 Preheat the oven to 375 degrees Fahrenheit. Beat the egg in a small bowl, and brush it over the loaf. Let dry for 10 minutes. Brush on a second coat of egg, and sprinkle with poppy seeds. Bake for 30 to 40 minutes until golden-brown. (The internal temperature should read 190 degrees F on an instant-read thermometer.)

Ham and Mushroom Quiche Bread Bowls

A quick version of quiche that doesn't require making and rolling out pastry, this recipe is perfect for breakfast, brunch or lunch. The ingredients for the filling can be adapted to make your own signature dish. For instance, try asparagus in the spring and roasted squash in the fall.

Serves 4

4 large bread rolls of approximately 4 inches
   in diameter
1 tsp. olive oil
1 Tbsp. butter
3 medium-sized mushrooms, thinly sliced (½ cup)
1 large shallot, thinly sliced (⅓ cup)
3 oz. Prosciutto or shaved deli ham,
   roughly chopped
¼ tsp. dried thyme
3 eggs
½ cup heavy cream
pinch of cayenne pepper
¼ tsp. fine sea salt
2 tsp. cornstarch
1 Tbsp. chopped parsley
3 Tbsp. finely shredded Parmesan cheese

1 Preheat the oven to 400 degrees Fahrenheit.

2 Slice the tops from the rolls, leaving a 1-inch base. Brush the tops with olive oil, and place cut-side up on a baking sheet.

3 Carefully cut the bread cuts perpendicularly to the edge to within about ¼ inch of the bottom without cutting through. Cut an X in the center without cutting all the way to the bottom, and dig out the interior bread with your fingers or a spoon. Save the bread to make breadcrumbs for another dish. Place the bread cups on the baking sheet.

4 In a small skillet, melt the butter. Add the mushrooms, shallot, prosciutto and thyme. Sauté until the mushrooms and shallot soften and the prosciutto becomes crispy. Save a few pieces of prosciutto for garnish.

5 Divide the rest of the filling among the cups. In a blender, process the eggs, cream, cayenne pepper, salt and cornstarch until smooth. Add the parsley, and pulse to mix. Pour the egg mixture over the filling in each of the bread bowls. Sprinkle with Parmesan cheese.

6 Bake for 20 minutes until set. Watch the toast tops, as they can brown too quickly and might need to be removed a few minutes earlier. Remove from the oven, and garnish with prosciutto.

A gift of a dozen eggs in beautiful blues, greens and browns began this egg project. With added respect for farm-fresh eggs, Patricia Lehnhardt explored the wonderful world of egg cookery with delicious results and a newfound love of the richness that they provide. She cooks, writes and photographs food in Galena, Illinois.

Sandwiches

RECIPES AND PHOTOS BY
PATRICIA LEHNHARDT

Eggs aren't just for breakfast, as sandwiches are not just for lunch. Egg sandwiches have found their way into almost every fast-food drive-through restaurant. There are so many other possibilities, as you will see here.

Egg Salad

Makes 2 sandwiches

3 eggs: hard-boiled, cooled and peeled
3 Tbsp. mayonnaise
1½ tsp. mustard
salt and pepper to taste
1 Tbsp. chopped chives

1 Coarsely chop the eggs, and place them in a bowl. Add the mayonnaise, mustard, salt, pepper and chives. Gently mix together. Serve on toast with lettuce and bacon.

Perfect hard-boiled eggs

Eggs that are at least 1 week old peel easier. Place a single layer of eggs on the bottom of a saucepan. Add cold water to cover by 1 inch. Cover, and bring to a boil. As soon as it reaches a full boil, turn off the heat, leaving on the lid and the pot on the burner. Set the timer for 12 minutes. Drain, and run cold water over the eggs to cool. Refrigerate until cold.

Variations

> Use your favorite mustard. I used Champagne dill. Dijon is traditional, but ballpark works just fine, too.

> Wonderful bread is key. Try whole-wheat toast; a croissant; rich, egg-y farmhouse bread; or rye. All are great!

> Add crunch and flavor with finely chopped celery or water chestnuts. Use only a couple of tablespoons so as not to distract from the eggs.

> Your choice of herbs can make a difference. Tarragon, dill or parsley all work well.

> Want a little more zip? Dill pickle relish adds some spark, or try sweet relish.

Croque Madame

The croque monsieur remains a French café staple of ham and cheese. Put a fried egg on top, and it becomes a croque madame. Unlike a regular grilled ham and cheese, the layer of Mornay sauce adds that certain *je ne sais quoi* that makes French cuisine so famous.

Serves 4

2 Tbsp. butter
2 Tbsp. all-purpose flour
1 cup milk
6 oz. (2 cups) grated cheese, such as Gruyère, Gouda
   or Swiss, divided
¼ cup finely grated Parmesan
salt and pepper to taste
pinch of nutmeg
8 slices artisan bread, toasted
2 Tbsp. Dijon mustard
8 thin slices of deli ham
2 Tbsp. canola oil
4 eggs

1 Preheat the broiler to high.

2 Melt the butter in a small saucepan. Add the flour, and whisk until smooth, cooking over low heat for 1 minute.

3 Pour in the milk, and continue whisking until the sauce is thick and smooth. Add ½ cup grated cheese and the Parmesan, salt, pepper and nutmeg. Stir until the cheese melts. Keep warm.

4 Lay 4 slices of toast on a baking sheet. Spread with mustard, and lay 2 slices of ham on each slice. Divide the remaining cheese over the ham. Broil until the cheese melts — 1 to 2 minutes.

5 Top with the remaining 4 slices of toast and a portion of the cheese sauce. Broil until the sauce begins to brown. Keep warm.

6 Heat the oil in a large skillet, and break in the eggs. Cook until the whites are opaque and the yolks are still runny. Transfer an egg onto the top of each sandwich, and serve warm.

Egg and Chorizo Waffle Sandwiches

This Southwest breakfast or brunch dish is sure to please the spicy eaters at your table. For a quicker version, use flour or corn tortillas in place of the waffles.

Makes 4 sandwiches

Crispy corn waffles
½ cup cornmeal
¼ cup all-purpose flour
¼ cup cornstarch
1 tsp. baking powder
1 cup chicken stock
¼ cup canola oil
1 large egg, separated
1 Tbsp. sugar

1. Preheat a regular waffle iron (not one for Belgian waffles).

2. In a small bowl, combine the cornmeal, flour, cornstarch and baking powder.

3. In another bowl, whisk together the chicken stock, oil and egg yolk.

4. In a third bowl, beat the egg white until soft peaks form. Add the sugar, 1 teaspoon at a time, beating until stiff and glossy.

5. Pour the wet ingredients into the dry ingredients, and whisk until combined. Fold in the egg white.

6. Bake on the iron, using about ½ cup batter per waffle. Leave in the iron for 1 extra minute after the timer sounds to make sure it is crisp. Transfer to a rack to cool while you bake the rest of the waffles.

Egg Chorizo Filling

8 oz. Mexican chorizo, casings removed
½ cup chopped onion
½ cup diced red bell pepper
6 eggs
2 Tbsp. chopped cilantro
¼ cup prepared salsa

1. In a medium frying pan, cook the chorizo, breaking it up as it browns.

2. Drain excess grease, and add the onion and pepper. Sauté until softened.

3. Beat the eggs in a bowl until fluffy. Add to the pan, and cook until just set, stirring gently.

4. Stir in the cilantro, and serve on a waffle with salsa drizzled over the filling and topped with another waffle.

Veggie Eggs in Pita

Make this quick breakfast or lunch using the vegetables you have on hand. Vary the flavoring and cheese to suit your desires; Italian, Mexican or Indian curry all taste delicious. If you're out of pita, use toast or tortilla wraps.

Serves 2

1 Tbsp. olive oil
⅓ cup diced onion
½ cup (3 medium) sliced mushrooms
¼ cup diced bell pepper
½ cup thinly sliced zucchini
1 cup baby spinach
2 eggs
¼ tsp. dried oregano
salt and pepper to taste
¼ cup crumbled feta cheese
1 pita bread, cut in half

1 Heat the olive oil in a medium skillet. Add the onion, mushrooms, pepper and zucchini. Sauté until everything is softened and beginning to brown around the edges.

2 Stir in the spinach, and cook until wilted — about 1 minute.

3 In a small bowl, beat the eggs with the oregano, salt and pepper.

4 Add the eggs to the vegetables, and cook until the eggs are set, stirring gently. Sprinkle the feta cheese on top. Stuff into 2 pita halves to serve.

A gift of a dozen eggs in beautiful blues, greens and browns began this egg project. With added respect for farm-fresh eggs, Patricia Lehnhardt explored the wonderful world of egg cookery with delicious results and a newfound love of the richness that they provide. She cooks, writes and photographs food in Galena, Illinois.

Soups

RECIPES AND PHOTOS BY
JUDITH HAUSMAN

Start with a good broth; then add a good egg. That simple formula equals a nourishing, comforting soup in many cuisines. A homemade chicken or vegetarian stock makes all the difference, but boxed or canned broth can be flavor-boosted before adding the egg. Bits of meat or vegetable can be cooked in the broth or used as garnishes. Rice or noodles can bulk up the soup, too.

Try to use fresh-farm eggs, and calculate about one-half egg per serving, except where the egg is cooked whole. In those soups, give every diner his or her own egg.

Avgolemono

This recipe for Greek comfort soup achieves a satiny texture by tempering the egg. You beat some of the hot broth into the egg before returning that mix to the pot. Feel free to add more greens, shredded chicken or even little meatballs.

Serves 4

3 cups homemade or high-quality chicken or vegetable broth
2 small carrots, thinly sliced
salt and pepper to taste
3 Tbsp. fresh lemon juice
2 eggs
¾ cup cooked rice or ½ cup uncooked orzo
a few chard or spinach leaves, sliced, or 1 handful of parsley, chopped to garnish (optional)

1 In a saucepan, simmer the stock long enough to cook the carrots — about 7 minutes. Season with salt and pepper to taste.

2 Meanwhile, squeeze the lemon juice into a measuring cup or bowl with a spout. Beat the eggs into the lemon juice.

3 When the carrots are cooked, beat 1 ladleful of hot soup into the egg-lemon mix until the mix is smooth. Then pour that mix into the soup pot in a steady stream, stirring the hot soup at the same time. Serve.

Stracciatella

This Italian soup is even easier because the egg is scrambled right in the broth. You'll get the hang of the pour-and-stir technique in no time. Use good-quality Parmesan.

Serves 4

4 cups homemade or high-quality chicken
   or vegetable broth
salt and pepper to taste
3 eggs
4 (or more) Tbsp. freshly grated Parmesan
2 Tbsp. parsley, chopped
2 Tbsp. basil, chopped
1 cup spinach, sliced, or 1 cup whole baby
   spinach leaves

1. In a saucepan, simmer and season the stock with salt and pepper.

2. In a bowl, beat the eggs, cheese and herbs.

3. Lower the heat on the stock. Drizzle the egg-cheese mix into the hot broth while you stir the broth slowly with a fork to form thin strands.

4. Stir in the spinach. Serve hot.

Ramen with Egg

Take this "kid food" up a level with a few easy additions. If you prefer, leave out the salty flavor pack altogether. Instead, spend another minute seasoning the noodles with a little garlic, soy sauce and ginger.

Serves 2

2 cups water
1 pack ramen noodles, any flavor
1 egg per serving

Garnish

1 scallion
1 handful cilantro, chopped
1 pinch red pepper flakes

1. In a saucepan, bring the water to a boil, and dissolve the contents of the flavor pack in it. Break up the noodles, and cook for 1½ to 2 minutes.

2. Break the egg(s) into a bowl, taking care not to break the yolk(s). Slip the egg(s) into the simmering soup, turn off the heat, and cover the pot for about 3 minutes.

3. When the egg(s) look clouded over and poached through, pour the soup into 2 bowls, garnish with scallion, cilantro and pepper flakes, and serve.

Egg Drop Soup

The technique here is just like in stracciatella, where you scramble the eggs in the broth. The flavors are similar to ramen, as are the possible additions.

Serves 4

4 cups homemade or high-quality chicken
   or vegetable broth
3 eggs
1 tsp. cornstarch

Flavorings
½-inch piece fresh ginger, peeled and sliced
1 star anise
1 stem lemongrass
1 Tbsp. soy sauce
1 cinnamon stick
salt and pepper to taste

Optional
½ cup finely diced extra-firm tofu

¾ cup mushrooms, sliced
1 small bunch baby bok choy, beet greens, spinach
   or chard, thinly sliced
3 scallions
½ cup shredded, cooked chicken or shrimp

1 In a medium pot, simmer the broth with one or all of the flavorings for about 12 to 15 minutes. Scoop the flavorings out of the broth with a slotted spoon. Season to taste with salt and pepper.

2 Break the eggs into a measuring cup or bowl with a spout, and beat them well with the cornstarch. Over very low heat, slowly pour the eggs into the hot broth while you stir the broth with a fork or whisk.

3 Add any optional items, cook for 1 minute to warm, and serve.

Judith Hausman lives in the lower Hudson Valley of New York, where she writes often about the region's food, farms and residents. As "The Hungry Locavore," her recipes appear weekly at www.urbanfarmonline.com

Egg Salad Express

RECIPES BY
LISA MUNNIKSMA
PHOTOS BY
SHANNON O'NEILL CREIGHTON

These four recipes prove egg salad is so much more than just messy mayo.

If you shudder at the thought of eating egg salad — goopy, messy sandwich filling that tastes too much like mayonnaise — you're not alone. Don't shun the humble egg salad until you've tried a few creative renditions of this versatile dish, though.

Egg salad might not be the sophisticated rave of top culinary talent, but hard-boiled eggs are surprisingly delicious with many combinations of ingredients. You can make yours farm-fresh, keep it healthy, incorporate cheese and yogurt, or go with pickled additions.

Hard-boiled Success

To have a great egg salad, you first need great hard-boiled eggs. There's a delicate balance between undercooking and overcooking.

You might be familiar with the green tint that egg yolks take on. According to Nancy Clark, an Iowa State University Extension Nutrition and Health program specialist, the green is the result of a reaction between sulfur in the egg white and iron in the egg yolk that's caused by overcooking.

An undercooked whole egg can be considered medium-boiled. This results in a gelatinous yolk, which is OK for some uses but not for egg salad.

Here's how I get my hard-boiled eggs just right. (Others might use a different technique; see page 48 for one example.)

1. Use a pot that will fit the number of eggs that you are cooking in one layer.

2. Place the eggs in the pot, and add cold water to cover the eggs by 1 to 2 inches.

3. Leave the pot uncovered. Let the water come to a boil over high heat.

4. Remove the pot from the heat when it starts boiling. Cover the pot. Set a timer for 16 minutes.

5. When your timer goes off, set up your cooling bowl. Put a few inches of cold water in a large bowl. Using a slotted spoon, fish the eggs out of the pot, and place them in the bowl. Cover the eggs with ice. This cold-water bath stops the cooking process quickly.

6. Let the bowl sit on the counter for 1 hour; then drain the water, and refrigerate or use the eggs.

Try out these 4 egg salad recipes — each using a dozen eggs and making about 6 servings — and get creative in developing your own.

BELT Sandwich

A BELT — bacon, egg, lettuce and tomato — sandwich is a delight of early summer. The perfect sandwich has to be timed just right when the hens are still laying a lot of eggs, the lettuce is starting to lose production and the tomatoes are starting to pick up production. Because I like BELTs so much, I wondered if this concept would translate well into an egg salad. The answer is yes.

Cooking the bacon in the oven on a broiler pan allows the drippings to drain away so the bacon becomes perfectly crispy for chopping. The parchment paper on top prevents the bacon from spattering as it cooks.

Use any kind of pickle that you prefer in this recipe — whichever you'd normally serve beside a BELT sandwich.

Serves 6 (2 eggs per person)

5 slices thick-cut bacon
12 hard-boiled eggs
leaves from 4 parsley sprigs, chopped
10 pickle slices, chopped
¼ cup mayonnaise

1 Preheat the oven to 350 degrees Fahrenheit. Arrange the bacon slices on a broiler pan. Cover with parchment paper, and bake until crispy — about 40 minutes. Let the bacon cool, and finely chop it.

2 In a large bowl, mash the eggs with a fork or potato masher.

3 Add all of the ingredients to the same bowl, and mix.

4 Refrigerate for 1 hour or longer, and serve on toast with lettuce and sliced tomato.

Cheery Curried Egg Salad

I call this recipe "cheery" because of its bright colors — yellow, orange, green, white and red. I like the combination of soft eggs with crunchy vegetables. Carrots and celery are in season in spring and fall while onions are stored year-round, so this is a versatile recipe appropriate for much of the year.

Serves 6 (2 eggs per person)

12 hard-boiled eggs
¼ cup (heaping) finely chopped carrot (about ½ carrot)
¼ cup finely chopped celery (about 2 stalks)
2 Tbsp. finely chopped sweet yellow onion
¼ cup (heaping) mayonnaise
1 tsp. yellow mustard
½ tsp. salt
1 Tbsp. curry powder
½ tsp. paprika

1 In a large bowl, mash the eggs with a fork or potato masher.

2 To the same bowl, add all of the remaining ingredients except the paprika, and mix.

3 Refrigerate for 1 hour or longer, and serve open-faced on toast with paprika sprinkled on top.

Herbed Egg Salad

This is a nice egg salad any time there are fresh herbs around. You can make this with dried herbs, too, by substituting dry for fresh at a ratio of 1 tsp. dry to 1 Tbsp. fresh, but it's just not the same. The lemon juice and plain Greek yogurt make a creamy, tangy replacement for the traditional mayonnaise, bringing out — rather than masking — the herbal taste.

Serves 6 (2 eggs per person)

12 hard-boiled eggs
1 Tbsp. finely chopped sage
1½ Tbsp. finely chopped parsley
1 tsp. finely chopped oregano
1 Tbsp. finely chopped chives
½ cup plain Greek yogurt
1½ tsp. lemon juice
salt to taste

1. In a large bowl, mash the eggs with a fork or potato masher.

2. To the same bowl, add all of the remaining ingredients, and mix.

3. Refrigerate for 1 hour or longer, and serve on a bed of salad greens.

Mediterranean Egg Salad

I am sold on most dishes involving feta cheese or capers, and this egg salad combining Mediterranean flavors is no different. There is no thick condiment holding this egg salad together besides the feta, and the liquid from the jar of capers binds it. Still, this is a more crumbly egg salad than you might expect, which is why serving it in a pita is ideal.

Serves 6 (2 eggs per person)

12 hard-boiled eggs
½ cup crumbled feta cheese
¼ cup finely chopped red onion
¼ cup finely chopped cucumber
2 Tbsp. capers
2 Tbsp. liquid from the jar of capers

1 In a large bowl, mash the eggs with a fork or potato masher.

2 Add all of the remaining ingredients to the same bowl, and mix, taking care not to smash the capers.

3 Refrigerate for 1 hour or longer, and serve with pita bread.

Freelance writer Lisa Munniksma cooks with farm-fresh eggs on a farm in Kentucky. She blogs weekly about agricultural news and opinions for Hobby Farms magazine at www.hobbyfarms.com/newshog and blogs very occasionally about farming and traveling around the world at www.freelancefarmerchick.com

Soufflés

RECIPES AND PHOTOS BY
FIONA GREEN

A soufflé is the perfect dish for a lazy Sunday morning when you feel creative and have time to spare. Use fillings sparingly so you don't weigh down the soufflé. Let the eggs take center stage while the fillings play a supporting role. For best results, use room-temperature eggs. Prepare your fillings in advance, and make sure the oven is preheated to 400 degrees Fahrenheit.

A soufflé might be considered a culinary work of art, so allow your guests to appreciate your masterpiece at its best, and serve it as soon as it is has been removed from the oven. You have about 4 minutes before it starts to deflate. While creating a soufflé might seem daunting, it is actually quite straightforward. The more you practice, the easier it becomes.

Tip: To ensure that your soufflés rise tall without spilling over, create a cylinder out of aluminum foil to avoid any spillage. Simply wrap the foil around the ramekins prior to placing them in the oven. Remember to grease the foil and sprinkle it with Parmesan cheese so the soufflé won't stick.

Three-cheese and Mixed Herb Soufflé

This recipe celebrates the wonderful combination of cheese and eggs with a subtle addition of mixed herbs, which take the dish from delicious to sublime. I used herbes de Provence, but you should feel free to experiment with the herbs of your choice. The quantities here will make 2 or 3 individual soufflés, depending on the size of your ramekins. I made 3 soufflés with my 3½-inch ramekins and 2 with my 4- and 4½-inch dishes.

Serves 2 or 3

¼ cup Parmesan cheese, grated
2 Tbsp. butter
2 Tbsp. all-purpose flour
½ cup milk
½ cup mozzarella cheese, grated
½ cup Gruyère cheese, grated
1 tsp. dried mixed herbs such as herbes de Provence
pinch of salt
pinch of pepper
2 egg yolks
4 egg whites
¼ tsp. cream of tartar

Tip: You can prepare the roux a day ahead, and refrigerate it until you are ready to use it.

1 Grease 2 or 3 ramekins, depending on their size. Coat the insides with the shredded Parmesan cheese; then refrigerate them until ready to use.

2 Preheat the oven to 400 degrees Fahrenheit.

3 Next prepare your soufflé base, or roux. In a small saucepan, melt the butter, add the flour, and stir well to combine. Continue stirring over low heat for approximately 2 minutes; then remove from heat.

4 Pour in the milk, and continue to stir until a thick sauce has formed. Stir in the grated cheeses, herbs, salt and pepper, and mix well until the cheeses have melted and are incorporated into the sauce.

5 Add the egg yolks to the roux. Stir well to combine.

6 In a medium bowl, combine the egg whites with the cream of tartar, and whisk by hand until stiff peaks have formed.

7 Add egg whites to the roux in 3 stages. Using a rubber spatula, mix in one-third of the egg whites to lighten the roux. Then gently fold in the second and final thirds until just combined. The batter should be light and fluffy.

8 Divide the egg mixture equally between the dishes. You should have just enough to fill the dishes to the top.

When they are full, gently run a clean index finger around the rim of the ramekin dishes to form a small trench. This will help prevent the soufflé mix from spilling over as it rises.

9 Place the ramekins on the middle shelf of the oven, and cook for 5 minutes at 400 degrees F.

10 Reduce the heat to 375 degrees F, and continue to cook for 15 to 20 minutes, depending on the size of the ramekins. The soufflés will puff up and start to brown on top. Avoid opening the oven door until the time is up, or your soufflés might fall. Your works of art will be ready to serve when the soufflés look lightly browned on top and a toothpick inserted into the centers comes out clean. Take care not to overcook!

11 Serve immediately with warm, buttery croissants.

Soufflé with Roasted Red Pepper and Canadian Bacon

This soufflé combines smoky, roasted peppers with juicy Canadian bacon for a flavor combination that is out of this world. If you feel adventurous, you can roast the peppers, but you can save time and achieve similar results with a store-bought version. While the recipe calls for mozzarella cheese, a staple in most homes, different cheeses can be used according to personal taste. As in the previous recipe, the quantities listed are sufficient for 2 or 3 individual soufflés, depending on the size of your ramekins.

Serves 2 or 3

¼ cup Parmesan cheese, grated
1 roasted red pepper
3 oz. Canadian bacon, chopped into very small pieces
2 Tbsp. butter
2 Tbsp. all-purpose flour
½ cup milk
1 cup mozzarella cheese, grated
pinch of salt
pinch of pepper
2 egg yolks
4 egg whites
¼ tsp. cream of tartar

1 Grease 2 or 3 ramekins, coat the insides with Parmesan cheese, and refrigerate until ready to use.

2 Use a blender to purée the roasted red pepper; then pour it into a small bowl. Add the chopped bacon, and set aside.

3 Preheat the oven to 400 degrees Fahrenheit.

4 In a saucepan, melt the butter, add the flour, and stir to combine well. Stir over low heat for 2 minutes; then remove from heat.

5 Pour in the milk, and continue to stir until a thick sauce has formed. Stir in the mozzarella, salt and pepper, and mix well until the cheese has been incorporated into the sauce.

6 Add the egg yolks to the sauce. Stir well to combine.

7 In a medium bowl, combine the egg whites with the cream of tartar, and whisk by hand until stiff peaks have formed.

8 Add the puréed pepper and Canadian bacon to the roux; mix well. Add about one-third of the egg whites. Then, using a rubber spatula, carefully fold in the remaining egg whites, taking care not to overmix.

9 Divide the egg mixture equally between 2 or 3 ramekins, and place them in the oven. Cook for 5 minutes at 400 degrees F. Then reduce the heat to 375 degrees F, and continue to cook for 15 to 20 minutes.

10 Serve immediately with a dollop of sour cream and some freshly buttered toast.

Fiona Green is a photographer and writer living in Keller, Texas, who balances her love of creating and eating delicious food with competitive running.

Appetizers

BY **SAMANTHA JOHNSON AND PAULETTE JOHNSON**
PHOTOS BY **DANIEL JOHNSON**
FOOD STYLING BY **PAULETTE JOHNSON**

Eggs: They're a fundamental part of our breakfast fare, but they're also a natural candidate for highlighting a course of appetizers. These four recipes feature an all-star cast of appetizer options that will be the talk of your next get-together.

Easy Deviled Eggs

There are so many appetizers to make with eggs, but deviled eggs are one of the most popular options. This quick and easy recipe for delicious deviled eggs adds a bit of fresh crunch. Yum!

Makes 10

5 eggs, hard-boiled (see pages 48 and 58 for instructions) and peeled
¼ cup mayonnaise
1 tsp. mustard
½ tsp. dried parsley flakes
½ tsp. chopped chives
⅛ tsp. cayenne pepper
black pepper to taste
1 orange bell pepper, chopped into ½-inch pieces
paprika (optional)

1 Slice the eggs in half lengthwise, and gently scoop out the yolks. Place the yolks in a small bowl, and mash well with a fork.

2 Add mayonnaise and mustard to the yolks, and mix thoroughly. Add parsley flakes, chives, cayenne pepper and black pepper, and mix.

3 Place the yolk mixture in a pastry bag or sealable bag. (If using a sealable bag, clip the corner so the mixture can be piped through the hole.) Pipe the yolk mixture into each egg white, filling the empty space.

4 Garnish each egg with a piece of bell pepper, and sprinkle with paprika if desired.

Perfectly Pleasant Pickled Eggs

There are lots of ways to make pickled eggs. Essentially, you need eggs, vinegar, salt and your desired spices. Here's our take on sweetly spicy pickled eggs. Apple cider vinegar and brown sugar will create a stronger-flavored solution, so opt for white sugar and white distilled vinegar if you prefer a milder taste. Some people like to add beets for vivid coloring.

A couple of notes: Food-safety experts recommend using only blemish-free hard-boiled eggs and sterilizing your jars prior to filling. Refrigerate and use within 7 days. Read up on the proper process for pickling eggs prior to making your first batch. The National Center for Home Food Preservation offers suggestions at nchfp.uga.edu/how/can_06/pickled_eggs.html

Makes 1 quart (8 eggs)

1 small onion, thinly sliced
1½ tsp. salt
¼ tsp. celery seed
¼ tsp. turmeric
¾ tsp. mustard seed
⅛ tsp. allspice
1⅓ cups apple cider vinegar or white distilled vinegar

1 cup sugar, white or brown
8 eggs, hard-boiled

1 In a saucepan, combine all the ingredients except the eggs, and bring to a boil. Simmer 5 to 7 minutes, stirring occasionally.

2 Place the eggs in a quart-sized jar. Add the liquid to completely cover the eggs.

3 Cover, and refrigerate. Season for at least 24 hours. Use within 7 days.

Egg and Broccoli Mini Quiche Muffins

Who doesn't love a quiche? Serve up these petite quiche muffins, and watch them disappear at your next gathering. The flavorsome combination of broccoli and Swiss sets the stage for deliciousness.

Makes 24 small quiche muffins

1 package refrigerated pie crust, or use homemade
4 small heads fresh broccoli, chopped into small pieces
8 oz. Swiss cheese, shredded
3 eggs, beaten
2 cups milk
2 tsp. dill weed
¼ tsp. garlic powder or 2 garlic cloves, minced
¼ tsp. salt

1 Preheat the oven to 400 degrees Fahrenheit. Place the pie crusts on a lightly floured surface; if making your own, roll the dough to a thickness of just under ⅛ inch.

2 Use a round 3-inch cookie cutter (you can also use a glass of that size) to make 24 circles in the dough.

3 Lightly grease the cups of a standard-size muffin tin, and place a pie-crust circle in each cup. Press down.

4 Into each muffin cup, add an equal amount of the chopped broccoli and the Swiss cheese so that both ingredients are evenly distributed.

5 Combine the eggs and milk in a mixing bowl. Add the dill, garlic and salt, and mix.

6 Add approximately 1½ Tbsp. of the liquid ingredients to each cup, pouring directly over the broccoli and Swiss cheese.

7 Bake for approximately 25 minutes. Serve warm.

Bacon, Egg and Cheese Delights

In a hurry but still need to feed a lot of people? These bacon, egg and cheese appetizers take the worry out of appetizer prep while giving you a super-yummy combination that will have everybody coming back for more.

Makes 36 crackers

6 eggs: hard-boiled (see pages 48 and 58 for instructions), peeled and chopped
½ cup mayonnaise
⅛ tsp. salt
⅛ tsp. garlic powder
3 tsp. yellow mustard
¼ tsp. dried basil
36 butter crackers
10 to 12 slices bacon, cooked and sliced into 1- to 1½-inch pieces
4 oz. Cheddar cheese, shredded

1 In a bowl, gently combine the eggs, mayonnaise, salt, garlic powder, yellow mustard and basil.

2 Place a small portion of the egg mixture on each cracker. Assemble the crackers on a large serving platter.

3 Top with a piece of bacon. Sprinkle Cheddar cheese on top of the bacon.

4 If desired, heat briefly in the oven (1 to 2 minutes at 350 degrees Fahrenheit) or microwave (just a few seconds) to slightly melt the cheese.

Samantha Johnson is the author of several books, including "The Beginner's Guide to Vegetable Gardening" (Voyageur Press). Paulette Johnson is a professional photographer and writer and enjoys cooking and gardening.

RECIPES AND PHOTOS BY
PATRICIA LEHNHARDT

Egg cookery is celebrated every year on World Egg Day, which occurs on the second Friday in October. Eggs are abundant and accessible around the globe, and cooks in every country have their own famous egg dishes. We celebrate four of those recipes here from France, Korea, Spain and Greece.

Spinach Soufflé

Often feared as temperamental, the soufflé is the quintessential French dish that always pleases. Basic, simple ingredients are combined to make something sweet or savory. This spinach version makes a memorable luncheon for special guests when served with a fresh green salad. (For two more savory soufflé recipes, see page 62.)

Serves 4 to 6

1 tsp. butter (for coating the baking dish) plus 3 Tbsp.
½ cup finely chopped onion
3 Tbsp. all-purpose flour
1 cup half-and-half
¼ tsp. ground nutmeg
salt and pepper to taste
1 Tbsp. finely grated Parmesan cheese (for coating the baking dish) plus ½ cup
1 cup chopped, cooked spinach (frozen works well)
3 eggs, separated

1 Preheat the oven to 400 degrees Fahrenheit. Prepare a 6-cup baking dish or pan with straight sides by rubbing 1 tsp. butter over the inside of the pan. Then sprinkle 1 Tbsp. Parmesan over the butter, moving the dish so the cheese adheres to the surface of the pan. This will help the soufflé "grab" onto the sides of the pan while it rises during baking.

2 In a medium saucepan, sauté the onion in 3 Tbsp. butter until softened. Whisk in the flour and cook, stirring constantly, for 1 minute.

3 Pour in the half-and-half, and continue to whisk until the mixture becomes thick and smooth. Season with nutmeg, salt and pepper.

4 Stir in the remaining Parmesan cheese and spinach. Remove from the heat, and cool for 5 minutes.

5 Whisk the eggs yolks into the cream base, 1 at a time, working quickly to prevent curdling.

6 In a medium bowl, beat the egg whites to form stiff peaks. Fold one-third of the whites into the spinach base. When the mixture looks lighter, fold in the remaining egg whites very gently. Pour into the baking dish.

7 Place the dish in the oven on a rack one-third of the way from the bottom. Reduce the heat to 375 degrees F. Bake for 35 to 40 minutes until the soufflé looks golden.

8 Serve immediately, as it will fall quickly once removed from the oven. It'll still be tasty but not as dramatic!

Greek Chicken Lemon Soup

Using egg yolks as a thickener for this soup creates an amazing, velvety texture. The splash of lemon at the end lifts the flavors that otherwise might be too rich. In a traditional avgolemono, the chicken is often served on the side. Here, I added it to the thickened broth to heat. To save time, a rotisserie chicken and boxed broth can be used in this recipe, but please squeeze your own lemon juice.

Serves 4

4 cups chicken stock
½ cup orzo or other small pasta
4 egg yolks
1 cup shredded, cooked chicken
2 Tbsp. fresh lemon juice
salt and pepper to taste
4 thin lemon slices to garnish
4 parsley sprigs to garnish

1 Bring the chicken stock to a boil in a medium saucepan. Add the orzo, and cook until almost tender — about 7 minutes. Set the stock-and-orzo mixture aside.

2 In a medium bowl, whisk the egg yolks until smooth and lighter in color. Continue to whisk the egg yolks while adding ¼ cup of boiling broth.

3 When the broth is completely incorporated, add another ¼ cup of broth. This will slowly warm the eggs without curdling them. Continue adding the stock in ¼-cup portions until you have reached 1 cup.

4 Switch the whisk to the pot of stock and orzo, and slowly pour the warm egg mixture into the broth, continuing to whisk until incorporated.

5 Add the chicken, and bring the soup just to a simmer, stirring frequently, for about 5 minutes. Do not boil. Turn off the heat, and stir in the lemon juice, salt and pepper. Serve warm with lemon slices and parsley to garnish if desired.

Tortilla Española

Although it's a favorite for Spanish tapas, I like to serve this easy egg dish for breakfast or lunch as a main dish with fruit or greens. It consists of eggs, potatoes and salt, along with a little oil and onion, and melds into such a delightful bite.

**Serves 6 for breakfast or lunch
or makes 24 appetizer portions**

2 Tbsp. olive oil
1 large russet potato, peeled and cut into ½-inch dice
  (2 cups)
½ cup chopped onion
5 eggs
1 tsp. salt
½ tsp. coarse salt for garnish

1 In an 8-inch nonstick skillet, heat the oil, and add the potato and onion. Stir to coat with oil.

2 Cover the skillet, and cook over medium-low heat until the potatoes pieces are soft but not brown — 10 to 15 minutes. Check occasionally to stir and make sure the potatoes do not brown. You might have to lower the heat.

3 Beat the eggs and salt in a medium bowl. Pour the mixture over the potatoes, stirring to make sure the eggs distribute evenly. Stir a couple of times to let the raw eggs flow onto the surface of the pan.

4 After 10 to 12 minutes, when the sides and bottom are golden-brown, place a plate over the pan, and flip it quickly so the tortilla lands on the plate.

5 Slide the tortilla back into the pan to brown the top. Cook until golden on the bottom and the eggs are cooked through — 3 to 4 minutes.

6 Slide onto a cutting board. Cool for 10 minutes, sprinkle with coarse salt, and cut. Serve warm or at room temperature.

Bibimbap

While this recipe may seem intimidating, each component can be prepared in advance and cooked at the last minute. The combination of flavors is well worth the effort! Feel free to substitute chicken or fish for the marinated beef, or use whatever vegetables you have on hand. It's a dish designed for leftovers and perfected with a fried egg on top. Traditionally, Korean bibimbap is served in piping hot, heavy stoneware bowls, which will crisp the rice on the bottom. You can achieve the same effect without the special bowls by browning the rice in an iron skillet.

Serves 4

Rice
1 cup long-grain rice
2 cups water
1 tsp. salt

1 Combine the rice, water and salt in a saucepan. Bring to a boil, lower the heat, cover, and simmer for 15 minutes. Turn off the heat, and leave covered on the burner for 5 minutes to steam. Fluff with a fork.

For crispy rice: Heat 2 Tbsp. peanut oil in a cast-iron skillet. Add the cooked rice, and press down to form a large cake. Cover, and cook over medium heat until crispy on the bottom — about 10 to 15 minutes.

Beef
1 lb. rib-eye steak
6 garlic cloves, minced (2 Tbsp.)
2 Tbsp. minced ginger
½ cup soy sauce
2 Tbsp. brown sugar
2 tsp. toasted sesame oil
2 scallions, minced

1 Place the beef in the freezer for 30 minutes to firm. Slice as thinly as you can.

2 In a medium-sized bowl, combine the beef with the garlic, ginger, soy sauce, brown sugar, sesame oil and scallions. Mix well. Cover, and refrigerate overnight.

3 When ready to serve: Heat a grill pan over high heat, and grill the beef in batches until medium-rare — about 3 minutes.

Sauce
6 Tbsp. Korean barbecue sauce or gochujang
1 Tbsp. toasted sesame oil
1 Tbsp. sesame seeds
1 Tbsp. brown sugar
hot sauce to taste

1 Mix in a small bowl.

Vegetables
3 tsp. peanut oil, divided
4 cups baby spinach
8 shiitake mushrooms, destemmed and thinly sliced
1 large carrot, cut into matchsticks
½ English cucumber, thinly sliced
1 cup bean sprouts, rinsed

1 In a large pan, heat 1 tsp. oil. Add the spinach, and cook until wilted, stirring constantly, for about 2 minutes. Transfer to a plate.

2 Add 1 tsp. oil to the pan, and sauté the mushrooms until tender. Transfer to the plate.

3 Add 1 tsp. oil to the pan, and sauté the carrots until crisp-tender. Transfer to the plate. The cucumber and bean sprouts don't need to be cooked.

Eggs
1 Tbsp. peanut oil
4 eggs
salt and pepper to taste

1 Wipe out the pan used for the vegetables, heat the oil, and break in the eggs. Cook over medium-low heat until the whites look opaque and the yolks reach your desired doneness (traditionally runny). Season with salt and pepper.

Assembly
1 Tbsp. sesame seeds for garnish

1 Divide the rice among 4 bowls. To each, add beef, vegetables and 1 fried egg. Drizzle with the sauce, or serve the sauce on the side, and sprinkle with sesame seeds.

A gift of a dozen eggs in beautiful blues, greens and browns began this egg project. With added respect for farm-fresh eggs, Patricia Lehnhardt explored the wonderful world of egg cookery with delicious results and a newfound love of the richness that they provide. She cooks, writes and photographs food in Galena, Illinois.

Gastropub

RECIPES BY
**NICHOLAS YOUNGINER
AND KEVIN FOGLE**

PHOTOS BY
KEVIN FOGLE

A term coined during the late 20th century, "gastropub" refers to a new breed of British pubs that served innovative, upscale food in a relaxed bar setting. Today, the gastropub phenomenon is a growing global trend. Patrons can find a wide range of culinary options highlighting local ingredients, like farm-fresh eggs, prepared in unique and exciting ways. Our gastropub-inspired recipes offer four original dinner options from fried-sausage-covered Scotch eggs to a classic white pizza featuring broiled eggs.

Seared Salmon with Duck Eggs in a Nest of Purple Sweet Potatoes

Duck eggs often can be found at farmers markets and health-food stores. Chicken or another type of egg can be used in place of duck eggs.

Makes 4 servings

½ gallon peanut or canola oil
4 purple sweet potatoes
4 5- to 7-oz. pieces of salmon
salt and pepper
2 tsp. olive oil, divided
3 Tbsp. chicken stock or water
2 Tbsp. prepared brown mustard
1 Tbsp. honey
2 Tbsp. cold butter, cut into 1-Tbsp. squares
4 duck eggs (or any type of egg)

1 In a Dutch oven or high-sided pot, preheat the oil to 350 degrees Fahrenheit.

2 Using a spiralizer or box grater, grate the sweet potatoes to create thin "noodles." Shape the potatoes into a rounded mass, and deep-fry for 3 to 5 minutes, creating a crispy nest shape. Set the fried potatoes on a paper-towel-covered plate to drain a bit and cool.

Time-saving Tip: Instead of making the sweet potato nest, you can use frozen curly fries prepared according to the package instructions.

3 Season the salmon with salt and pepper.

4 Add 1 tsp. olive oil to a sauté pan, and bring to medium-high heat. Sear the salmon until crispy, browned and medium inside, flipping once, for approximately 6 to 8 minutes.

5 Remove the salmon from the pan. Keeping the pan on medium-high heat, pour in the stock, and stir to pick up the browned bits from cooking the salmon. Add the mustard and honey, and stir to combine. Reduce the liquid for approximately 3 minutes.

6 Whisk in the butter, 1 square at a time, making sure to continue whisking while adding. Add the second square once the first looks almost completely melted and incorporated into the sauce. Once the butter is incorporated and the sauce has thickened a bit, turn off the heat, and reserve the sauce.

7 In a small sauté pan over medium heat, add 1 tsp. olive oil, and crack in the eggs. Season with salt and pepper, and cook until the whites are set and the yolk is still runny — approximately 3 to 5 minutes.

8 To serve, place the fried egg on the sweet potato nest, and pour the sauce over the salmon next to the nest.

Scotch Eggs with Arugula Salad

Scotch eggs are popular at British-style pubs in the United States and often come with something on the side, such as a dipping sauce, or, in this case, a lightly dressed salad.

Makes 4 servings (2 eggs each)

8 eggs
1 tsp. sage, minced
2 tsp. chives, minced
½ tsp. cayenne pepper
½ tsp. ground nutmeg
3 cups ground sausage of your choice, such as
   breakfast or spicy Italian
4 Tbsp. flour
2 eggs, beaten
1 cup breadcrumbs
½ gallon vegetable oil
2 Tbsp. lemon juice
4 Tbsp. olive oil
3 cups baby arugula

1. Place the eggs in boiling water for 3 to 4 minutes. Then transfer the eggs to a bowl of cold water. When they are cool, peel them.

2. Combine the sage, chives, cayenne pepper and nutmeg with the sausage, and mix together. Shape the sausage into 8 oval-shaped patties of approximately 4 inches long.

3. Prepare a breading station by placing the flour, beaten eggs and breadcrumbs in 3 separate vessels. In a Dutch oven, preheat the oil to 325 degrees Fahrenheit.

4. Roll each peeled egg in flour. Place each egg on top of a sausage patty. Form the sausage around the egg, fully encasing it in a thin, even layer of sausage.

5. Roll each sausage-encased egg in flour, dip it into the beaten eggs, and cover it in breadcrumbs.

6. Add 4 sausage-encased eggs per batch, and fry for 4 minutes or until golden-brown. To check for doneness, cut open one egg to ensure the sausage is fully cooked. Repeat with the remaining eggs and sausage.

7. In a small bowl, whisk together the lemon juice and olive oil. Add the dressing to the arugula, and serve with the fried Scotch eggs.

Fontina, Leek and Broiled Egg Pizza

The arugula topping adds an interesting flavor and healthful aspect to this pizza. Purchase store-bought dough to speed up the cooking for a weeknight meal.

Makes 2 14-inch pizzas

3½ cups flour
1 tsp. sugar
1 packet (¼ oz.) instant-dry yeast
2 tsp. salt
1½ cups warm water (about 100 degrees Fahrenheit
   or slightly cooler)
2 Tbsp. olive oil
1 bunch leeks
1 ½ cups ricotta cheese
1 Tbsp. granulated garlic
2 cups fontina cheese, grated (or any white, melting
   cheese that you prefer)
8 eggs
salt and pepper to taste
2 tsp. butter
½ cups baby arugula

1 To prepare the pizza dough: To the bowl of a stand mixer, add the flour, sugar, yeast and salt. Mix on slow speed to combine the ingredients.

2 With the mixer still on slow, pour in the warm water and olive oil. Increase the mixer's speed to medium, and mix until the dough comes together and forms a ball, and the sides of the mixer are clean.

Time-saving Tip: Instead of making your own, purchase premade pizza dough. Many bakeries and grocery stores sell fresh pizza dough, which is often better.

If the pizza dough seems too sticky, add more flour, 1 Tbsp. at a time, until the dough pulls away cleanly from the mixer bowl.

3 Remove the dough ball into a bowl, cover with plastic wrap, and place in a warm, dark place for approximately 1 hour or until the dough has almost doubled in volume.

4 Once risen, remove the dough to a lightly floured work surface, and divide into 2 equal-sized pieces. Let rest at room temperature for approximately 10 minutes.

5 Preheat the oven to 500 degrees Fahrenheit.

6 Cut the white part of the leeks from the green leaves, thinly slice the white parts, discarding the green parts, and set aside.

7 Roll the dough into 14-inch rounds, and transfer the rounds to pizza stones or other flat cooking vessels.

8 Spread a thin layer of ricotta over the dough, and sprinkle the granulated garlic over that. Spread the fontina evenly over the pizza, covering the ricotta.

9 Create 4 small wells in the cheese, and crack an egg into each well. Season each egg with salt and pepper. Sprinkle the leeks over the pizza. Repeat all of the toppings on the other pizza.

10 Put the pizzas into the hot oven until the cheese is melted, the crust is crispy, and the eggs are cooked — approximately 15 minutes. Serve the pizzas with a garnish of fresh arugula over the top.

S_PHOTO /SHUTTERSTOCK

Steak with Potato Fritters and Sauce Béarnaise

You can create your own fritters using grated potatoes, or try making quick fritters (below) to save time while maintaining the flavor and texture of crispy potatoes.

Makes 4 servings

1 small shallot, diced into ⅛-inch pieces
1 Tbsp. finely chopped tarragon
2 tsp. + 1 tsp. black pepper
2 Tbsp. white wine
salt and pepper to taste
4 egg yolks
1 Tbsp. lemon juice
1 stick butter (8 Tbsp.), melted
1 Tbsp. water
pinch of salt
½ Tbsp. olive oil
1 gallon peanut or canola oil
2 large russet potatoes, peeled
4 Tbsp. flour
¼ tsp. cayenne pepper
4 6- to 8-oz. ribeye steaks (or any cut that you prefer)
1 Tbsp. butter

1 Heat a small saucepan over medium heat. Add the olive oil, shallot, tarragon and 2 tsp. black pepper. Once the shallots are soft and translucent, add the white wine, and stir the contents of the pan to loosen any browned bits. Reduce until the contents are nearly dry (approximately 3 to 5 minutes), and set aside.

2 To prepare the Béarnaise sauce using the **quick-blender method:** In a blender, combine the egg yolks and lemon juice. Pulse for about 15 seconds or until the yolks and lemon juice look thoroughly mixed and slightly lightened in color.

3 Heat the water in the microwave for 1 minute.

4 Turn on the blender containing the egg-and-lemon mixture, and stream in the hot butter. Then stream in the hot water. Add the pinch of salt and already-prepared shallot reduction, and pulse to combine. **Note:** The egg yolks will not be fully cooked, so you may want to use pasteurized eggs. (See page 19.)

5 To prepare the fritters: In a Dutch oven or high-sided pot, heat the oil to 350 degrees Fahrenheit.

6 While the oil heats, use a stand or hand mixer on medium-high speed to blend the egg whites until medium peaks form — approximately 4 minutes.

7 Remove the steaks from the refrigerator approximately 30 minutes before cooking to allow them to come to room temperature. Season the steaks liberally with salt and ground black pepper.

8 If not making the quick fritters (below left), grate the potatoes on the smallest side of a box grater, creating thin strips. Mix the egg whites with the grated potato and flour, adding the cayenne pepper and salt and pepper to taste.

9 Use a small ice-cream scoop or spoon to add 1 to 2 Tbsp. of the potato mixture to the fryer, and fry in the oil until crispy and brown — 4 to 5 minutes. Remove to a paper-towel-covered plate, and repeat with the remaining potato mixture.

10 Place a pan over high heat and, when hot, add 1 Tbsp. butter. Once the butter is melted, place the steaks in the pan, and cook for about 3 minutes on each side for medium-rare. Remove the steaks from the pan, and let them rest for 5 to 10 minutes before serving.

11 Plate a steak with several potato fritters and a small vessel of Béarnaise sauce, and serve immediately.

- -

Nicholas Younginer is a trained chef and nutritional anthropologist based in South Carolina. Kevin Fogle is a freelance writer and photographer also located in South Carolina.

Quick Fritters

2 cups frozen, shredded potatoes
2 eggs, whisked
1 Tbsp. vegetable oil
salt and pepper to taste

Combine the potatoes and eggs in a bowl. Add the vegetable oil to a frying pan over a medium burner, and heat. Place several scoops (about 2 Tbsp. in size) of the potato mixture in the pan, and cook for 2 or 3 minutes per side until browned. Season with salt and pepper; serve immediately.

Vegetarian

RECIPES AND PHOTOS BY **KYRA KIRKWOOD**

Eggs form the healthy backbone of these vegetarian dishes.

Browned Butter Pasta and Eggs

While pasta and eggs don't necessarily sound like an ideal combination, the resulting dish may surprise you. Eggs add a welcome bit of savory protein to a carb-heavy dish. The garlic and butter incorporate richness, making this pasta reminiscent of a less-healthy, but oh-so-good, shrimp scampi. Best yet: The whole dish can be whipped up in minutes, making weeknight meal planning a snap even when you haven't been to the grocery store this week.

Serves 4

8 oz. whole-wheat spaghetti
1 cup butter (salted or unsalted, depending on
   preference)
5 garlic cloves, minced
4 eggs
black pepper to taste
grated Parmesan cheese to taste
fresh flat-leaf parsley, coarsely chopped

1 Cook the pasta according to the package directions, stirring occasionally until the noodles are al dente. Drain the pasta when done, reserving ½ cup of the pasta water. Set aside.

2 In a large skillet, melt the butter over medium heat. Add the garlic, and sauté for 1 minute or so until the butter begins to brown.

3 Crack the eggs 1 at a time into the butter, and lightly scramble until thoroughly cooked. This should take about 3 minutes.

4 Add the spaghetti and reserved pasta water, and toss everything until lightly coated and mixed. Liberally sprinkle with Parmesan and a bit of pepper, and toss again.

5 Divide between 4 plates, add more Parmesan if desired, scatter the parsley on top, and serve.

Vegetarian Fried Rice with Vegetables

Fried rice gets a healthy spin in this vegetarian recipe. The salty bite of the soy sauce and the creaminess of the eggs mix perfectly with the array of crunchy vegetables and chewy brown rice. This can serve as a tasty side dish or a filling main course.

Serves 2 to 4

25 young, thin asparagus stems
3 Tbsp. coconut oil, divided
1 small onion, chopped
2 garlic cloves, minced
1 cup coarsely chopped mushrooms
½ small bell pepper, chopped
1 small zucchini, chopped
3 large eggs, beaten
2 cups cooked short-grain brown rice
½ tsp. powdered ginger
3 tsp. soy sauce
2 tsp. toasted sesame oil
pepper to taste

1   Trim the asparagus into 1-inch pieces, and lightly steam until tender. Set aside.

2   Heat a wok or large skillet over medium-high heat, and add 2 Tbsp. oil. Add the chopped onion and garlic, and sauté for 30 seconds. Then add the mushrooms, bell pepper and zucchini, stirring frequently until the vegetables are lightly browned and slightly soft.

3   Add the eggs and steamed asparagus, and cook until the eggs are cooked but not runny. Transfer all of this to a bowl, and set aside.

4   Add the remaining oil to the same wok, and heat. Add the cooked rice, ginger and soy sauce. Stir-fry until heated completely through.

5   Return the vegetable-and-egg mixture to the pan, and add the sesame oil and pepper. Toss very well, and cook until everything is heated through and mixed — about 1 minute. Transfer to a platter, and serve hot.

- -

When not creating recipes, Kyra Kirkwood writes books, teaches journalism and spends time with her husband and children. Visit her at www.kyrakirkwood.com

RECIPES BY CHERYL MORRISON

PHOTOS BY FIONA GREEN

Sweet custards often work behind the scenes as pie fillings, ice cream bases and the silky deliciousness between cake layers. But custards on their own make outstanding desserts, providing smooth finishes to even the most elegant dinners. They require few ingredients other than eggs yolks, cream and sugar, and you can make them a day or two in advance.

Caramel Custard

This simple dessert will produce appreciative sounds around your dinner table ... followed by requests for the recipe. The custard is delicious all by itself, but adding whipped cream, chocolate shavings and salt flakes can make it even more appealing.

Makes 4 servings

1 pint heavy cream
½ vanilla bean
1 Tbsp. water
½ cup plus 1 Tbsp. granulated sugar
3 egg yolks
pinch of table salt

whipped cream (optional)
1 oz. bittersweet chocolate shavings (optional)
4 pinches of Maldon or other flaky sea salt (optional)

1 Preheat the oven to 300 degrees Fahrenheit.

2 Pour the cream into a medium saucepan. Slit the half-vanilla bean lengthwise, scrape its seeds into the cream, and add the scraped pod to the cream.

3 With the pan over medium heat, bring the cream almost to a boil; then remove it from the heat, and set it aside.

4 In a small saucepan, add the water to the ½ cup sugar, and bring it to a boil, stirring constantly

until the sugar is dissolved. Continue boiling the mixture for a few minutes, swirling the pan and brushing the sugar from the sides with a moistened pastry brush a few times. When the mixture takes on a deep caramel color, remove it from the heat.

5 After removing and discarding the vanilla pod, slowly add the hot sugar mixture to the cream. Simmer the cream for about 2 minutes, stirring it occasionally, until the color is evenly distributed and the mixture is smooth.

6 In a medium-sized bowl, whisk the egg yolks with the table salt and 1 Tbsp. sugar until they are blended. Continue whisking while slowly adding the cream mixture.

7 Divide the custard between 4 6-oz. ovenproof dishes. Place the dishes in a glass or ceramic baking pan, and add water to the pan until it reaches about halfway up the sides of the custard dishes.

8 Bake the custard for about 1 hour. When the custard is set at the edges but its center still wobbles, remove the dishes from the pan, and set them on a wire rack to cool.

9 Chill them uncovered in the refrigerator for at least 3 hours.

10 Just before serving, garnish each dish with a dollop of whipped cream, chocolate shavings and a pinch of flaked salt.

Lemon Crème Brûlée

For all of its sophistication, crème brûlée is easy to make. Adding the thin crust of sugar that distinguishes a crème brûlée from other custards is a little easier with a small culinary blowtorch, but you can achieve the same result with a broiler.

Makes 4 servings

1 lemon (1 Tbsp. zest + ½ tsp. juice)
½ vanilla bean
1½ cups heavy cream
5 Tbsp. sugar, divided
pinch of table salt
3 egg yolks
lemon peel slices for optional garnish
blueberries for optional garnish

1 Preheat the oven to 325 degrees Fahrenheit, placing a rack on the middle level.

2 Finely grate 1 Tbsp. zest from the lemon, taking only the yellow part of the rind and avoiding the white underneath.

3 Pour the cream into a medium saucepan, and add the lemon zest, 3½ Tbsp. sugar and the salt. Make a lengthwise slit in the half-vanilla bean, scrape its seeds into the cream, and add the pod. Stir the cream occasionally as you slowly heat it. When it is almost at the boiling point, remove it from the heat.

4 In a medium bowl, whisk the egg yolks; then gradually whisk the hot cream into the yolks.

5 Strain the mixture through a fine sieve over a large glass measuring cup or a bowl with a pouring spout; then stir in ½ tsp. juice from the lemon that you already zested. Discard the vanilla pod and any lemon zest that you caught in the strainer.

6 Divide the liquid mixture between 4 6-oz. baking dishes. Place the dishes in a large glass or ceramic baking pan, and add water to the pan until it reaches about halfway up the sides of the baking dishes.

7 Bake the custard for 30 to 35 minutes until it is set at the edges but still jiggles in the center of the dish. Remove the pan from the oven. Let the custards cool in their water bath for approximately 20 or 30 minutes. Then remove them from the pan, and set them uncovered in the refrigerator for at least 4 hours to chill and firm.

8 Sprinkle about 1 teaspoon sugar evenly over each dish of chilled custard; then caramelize the sugar coating. You can do this by holding a blowtorch flame close to the sugar and moving it evenly back and forth or by setting the dishes on a baking sheet and placing them under a broiler as close to the flame as possible. Either way, watch closely to make sure the sugar caramelizes without burning.

9 Let the caramelized sugar harden for at least 5 minutes before serving. A thin slice of lemon peel and a few blueberries serve well as a garnish.

- -

Cheryl Morrison frequently makes and serves custard-based desserts at her homes in New York City and southern Vermont.

IRYNA DENYSOVA/SHUTTERSTOCK

Desserts

RECIPES AND PHOTOS BY
JEN NATHAN ORRIS

While both the egg white and yolk are necessary for most standard egg dishes, the parts are mightier than the whole when it comes to dessert. The yolk is important for creamy desserts like lemon curd and key lime pie. Farm-fresh eggs give these citrus delights a rich and creamy texture and provide a sunny yellow color. The whites, while finicky in the mixing bowl, are reliable in the pan, as proven by these easy meringue cookies.

The key to many egg desserts is patience. Meringues in particular require a no-peeking policy. The same goes for the key lime pie's refrigeration stage. Opening and shutting the refrigerator door can cause cracks in the filling. Lemon curd is more forgiving, but letting it cool overnight improves its flavor.

Forgotten Meringues

This recipe harkens back to my grandmother's recipe box. The original card is covered in her loopy script, and my mother's changes are written in pencil along the margin. A few steps have been clarified, but otherwise these chocolate chip meringues are left unchanged since the 1960s. It's hard to wait overnight for these cookies to settle, but opening up the oven in the morning brings a sweet reward. They may keep the moniker "forgotten," but they are always anticipated.

Makes 24 meringues

1 tsp. vanilla
2 egg whites
½ cup sugar
¼ tsp. cream of tartar
1 cup chocolate chips

1 Preheat the oven to 350 degrees Fahrenheit. In a medium bowl, beat the vanilla with the egg whites just until firm.

2 Add the sugar and cream of tartar gradually (one spoonful at a time), and beat until very stiff. Stir in the chocolate chips.

3 Drop the mixture in dollops onto a baking sheet lined with parchment paper.

4 Place in the preheated oven, and immediately turn off the oven. Leave in the closed oven overnight or for 10 hours.

Gingersnap Key Lime Pie

Tart is the name of the game when it comes to key lime pie. Swapping a slew of tiny key limes for presqueezed lime juice is just as tasty as the original. Pulsing the gingersnaps in the blender or food processor ensures a crumbly texture. Bake the crust in advance, and let it cool completely to make sure the filling sets correctly.

Makes 1 8-inch pie

Crust
½ cup crushed gingersnap cookies
2 Tbsp. brown sugar
¼ tsp. salt
¼ cup melted butter

Filling
4 egg yolks
1 14-oz. can sweetened condensed milk
½ cup lime juice

1 Preheat the oven to 350 degrees Fahrenheit.

2 Combine the gingersnaps, brown sugar and salt in a medium bowl. Stir in the melted butter, and mix until thoroughly combined.

3 Press into an 8-inch pie pan. Bake for 8 minutes. Allow to cool completely.

4 Meanwhile, in another bowl, beat the egg yolks with the condensed milk. Add the lime juice, and mix thoroughly.

5 Pour the filling into the pie crust. Let it settle for 2 minutes.

6 Bake in the oven for 15 minutes. Let cool completely, and refrigerate for 8 hours or overnight.

Lemon Curd

Lemon curd, whether a gift or a homemade treat, is always welcome. There are myriad uses for this tangy treat. Slather it on donut holes, layer it between pancakes, or use it as a filling in the crepes on page 95.

Makes 1 pint (about 4 servings)

4 egg yolks
1 cup sugar
⅓ cup lemon juice
¼ cup butter, cut into small pieces
1 tsp. lemon zest
pinch of salt

1 Fill a large saucepan with 1 to 2 inches of water, and bring to a very low simmer.

2 Combine the egg yolks, sugar and lemon juice in a medium-size heat-safe bowl.

3 Place the bowl over the simmering water in the saucepan, and whisk the curd constantly for 8 to 10 minutes.

4 Remove the bowl from the heat, and fold in the butter until fully incorporated. Add the lemon zest and salt, and mix until just combined.

5 Strain the curd through a fine-mesh strainer, and refrigerate for 4 hours or overnight.

Tip: Place a piece of plastic wrap over the curd before refrigerating to prevent skin from forming.

Easy Crepes

Crepes can contain endless possibilities. Fill them with bananas and peanut butter, fresh berries or the lemon curd on page 93.

Makes 6 to 8 crepes

1 Tbsp. butter
2 eggs
1 cup flour
1¼ cups whole milk
2 tsp. sugar
1 Tbsp. salt

1 Melt the butter in an 8-inch pan. Set aside.

2 Whisk the eggs and flour in a large mixing bowl. Slowly add the milk, followed by the sugar, salt and melted butter.

3 Pour into a blender, and pulse until frothy. Let sit for 5 minutes, or refrigerate overnight.

4 Pour ¼ cup batter into a greased crepe pan or 10-inch frying pan. Swirl lightly, and cook until the edges brown.

5 Flip with a spatula, and remove from the pan after 1 minute.

6 Spoon the filling of your choice into the center, and fold.

7 Repeat with the rest of the batter, greasing the pan before each crepe.

Jen Nathan Orris is a writer and homesteader from Asheville, North Carolina. She lives on a five-acre property with her husband, two dogs and seven chickens.

recipe index

PATRICIA LEHNHARDT

JEN NATHAN ORRIS